The Right Way for Small Business [3 in 1]

Make Your Business Model Come to Life. Use the Best Tools to Get Low-Cost Customers and Win the Competition with Originality

By

Nespy Online Marketing

for clarifying purposes only and are the owned by the owners themselves, not affiliated with this document.

Author: Nespy Online Marketing

THE GOLDEN
INNER CIRCLE

The Golden Inner Circle is an elitist group business incubator. It's a way to speed yourself up with far fewer setbacks. If you are already on track follow these enlighten entrepreneurs to take you to the next level of your potential.

Get the support you need to:

- free yourself from negative limiting beliefs

- develop a marketing strategy that works

- discover the Golden Method to improve your skills

- realize the dream of being able to work in complete autonomy

- create passive income with low-budget investments form your home.

The Golden Inner Circle is the movement that is leading hundreds of people to find a real strategy to achieve great results in the most profitable businesses such as Youtube, Instagram, Airbnb...

This series of over 20 books called "Clever Entrepreneurs in the XXI Century" is a step-by-step program that will take you from zero to the highest level of success.

The information contained within will help you to raise the dormant leader inside you, develop the King Midas' touch and to embody the NEW Golden YOU.

Table of Contents

Dropshipping Business Model on a Budget

Youtube, Tik-Tok and Instagram Made Easy

<u>The 9+1 Best Home-Based Business Model of 2021</u>

Dropshipping Business Model on a Budget

The Risk-Low E-Com Guide to Create Your Online Store and Generate Profits with less than 47$

By

Nespy Online Marketing

Table of contents

Exit LADY JANE GREY.

HENRY
Time for a drink?

JOHN
Just a few more. Who's that?

HENRY
It's Rosaline.

JOHN
Ah, from *Love's Labor's Lost*.

HENRY
No.

JOHN
Oh, from *Love's Labor's Won*.

HENRY
No, from *Romeo and Rosaline*.

[PROJECTION: The Villa of the Capulets, Verona]

JOHN
I don't think so...that can't be.

HENRY
Yes, she's Romeo's first crush...remember?

JOHN
Absolutely not.

Introduction

With very little startup expenses, dropshipping is an innovative business model.

A dropshipping business is where an owner finds a collection of distributors to deliver and offer goods for their website. However, as in an e-commerce business, instead of owning the merchandise, a third party does much of the distribution and logistics for them. That third party is usually a wholesaler, who on behalf of the business "dropships" the consumer's goods.

When you start a retail shop, there are several factors to consider, but among the most significant aspects, you have to decide whether you'd like to store inventory or have a wholesale distributor. You must purchase goods in bulk, stock, unpack and send them to customers of your products if you want to store inventory. You may, therefore, contract the phase of storing, packaging and exporting to a drop-ship supplier by picking a wholesale distributor. As direct fulfillment, a drop-ship supplier is often described, but both definitions may be used to define the same service.

The wholesaler, who usually manufactures the product, delivers the product at the most basic, any time anyone buys a product, and you get a part of the sale for the product marketing.

Unless the client puts an order for it, you don't pay for the thing.

Dropshipping is an internet-based business model that draws novices and experts alike to choose a niche, create a b
money, with probabl

OTHER WOMEN

with Rosaline before he meets

sick over her...

draft...

er?

re fast...

letter from HENRY, who becomes Mercutio.)

! Too well I know the hand.
m that Montague?
Mock not my grief,
great flood of sugared words,
ses and these tortured rhymes
evotion unto death,
ve, are most intolerable!
yours, this Romeo,
do not now deny it,
thee in Verona's streets
this spaniel and his pack

Chapter 1. What is Dropshipping?

Dropshipping is a retail model of e-commerce that enables retailers to offer goods without maintaining any physical inventory. The company sells the product to the buyer through dropshipping and sends the purchase order to a third-party seller, who then delivers the order directly on behalf of the retailer to the customer. Dropshipping sellers may not need to spend in any commodity stock, inventory or storage room and do not manage the phase of fulfillment.

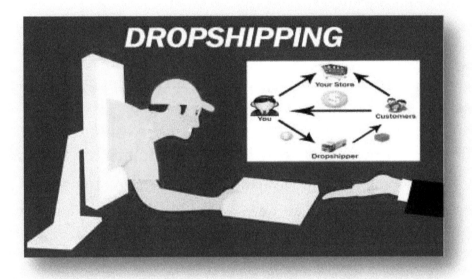

Dropshipping is a form of retail fulfillment, where the goods are ordered from a third-party retailer instead of a store stocks products. The goods are then delivered directly to the customer. This way, the vendor doesn't have to personally manage the product. A familiar sound? Maybe not, but dropshipping is a fulfillment model utilized by 35 percent of online stores.

This is mostly a hands-off process for the store. The retailer doesn't have to buy stock or, in any manner, meet the orders. The third-party retailer, instead, takes control of the product itself.

For startups, dropshipping is great since it does not take as much as the conventional sales model. You don't have to prepare, pay overhead, & stock merchandise in a brick-and-mortar store. Instead, you start an online shop to purchase bulk goods and warehouse space from vendors that already have products.

In dropshipping, the merchant is solely responsible for attracting clients and handling orders, ensuring you'll be a middleman effectively. Despite this, through pricing up the goods you offer, you can gain the lion's share of the profits. It's an easy model of business, so one that can be really successful.

Millions of entrepreneurs switch to dropshipping to get started because it takes less hassle and capital. That's why you're probably interested. And the best of all news? Through dropshipping, you can create a company right from your laptop that is profitable in the long term.

There are several pitfalls and benefits, of course, and it is essential that we check at them before you launch your own e-commerce dropshipping firm. However, once you realize the positives and negatives of dropshipping, it'll be a breeze to learn how to do so effectively.

1.1 Benefits of dropshipping

For aspiring entrepreneurs, dropshipping is a smart business move to start with, which is accessible. You can easily evaluate multiple business concepts with a small downside with dropshipping, which helps you to think a lot about how to pick and sell in-demand goods. Here are a couple more explanations why dropshipping is a popular business.

1. Little capital is required

Perhaps the greatest benefit to dropshipping is that an e-commerce website can be opened without needing to spend thousands of dollars in stock upfront. Typically, retailers have had to bundle up large quantities of inventory with capital investments.

For the dropshipping model, unless you have already made the transaction and have been charged by the consumer, you may not have to buy a product. It is possible to start sourcing goods without substantial up-front inventory investments and launch a profitable dropshipping company with very little capital. And since you are not committed to sales, as in a typical retail sector, there is less chance of launching a dropshipping shop through any inventory bought up front.

2. Easy to get started

It's also simpler to operate an e-commerce company because you don't have to interact with physical products. You don't have to take stress with dropshipping about:

- Paying for a warehouse or managing it
- Tracking inventory for any accounting reasons
- Packing & shipping your orders
- Continually ordering products & managing stock level
- Inbound shipments and handling returns

3. Low overhead

Your overhead expenses are very minimal, and you don't have to deal with buying inventory or maintaining a warehouse. In reality, several popular dropshipping stores are managed as home-based enterprises, needing nothing more to run than a laptop & a few operational expenses. These costs are likely to rise as you expand but are still low relative to standard brick-and-mortar stores.

4. Flexible location

From almost anywhere via an internet connection, a dropshipping company can be managed. You can operate and manage the business as long as you can effectively connect with vendors and consumers.

5. Wide selection of goods to sell

Because you don't really have to pre-purchase any items you market, you can offer your potential clients a variety of trending products. If an item is stored by vendors, you will mark it for sale at no added cost at your online store.

6. Easier for testing

Dropshipping is a valuable form of fulfillment for both the opening of a new store and also for company owners seeking to measure consumers' demand for additional types of items, such as shoes or whole new product ranges. Again, the primary advantage of dropshipping is the opportunity to list and likely sell goods before committing to purchasing a significant quantity of stock.

7. Easier to scale

For a traditional retail firm, you would typically need to perform three times as much work if you get three times the amount of orders.

By using dropshipping vendors, suppliers would be liable for more of the work to handle extra orders, helping you to improve with fewer growth pains & little incremental work.

Sales growth can often bring extra work, especially customer service, however companies which use dropshipping scale especially well comparison to standard e-commerce businesses.

8. Dropshipping starts easily.

In order to get started, you need not be a business guru. You don't really require some past company knowledge, honestly. You will get started easily and learn the rest while you move along if you spend some time to learn its basics.

It is too easy to drop shipping, and it takes so little from you. To help you out, you don't need a warehouse to store goods or a staff. You don't need to think about packaging or storage either. You do not even have to devote a certain period of time in your shop every day. Surprisingly, it's hands-off, especially once you get underway.

All of this means that today you can begin your company. Within a matter of hours, you will begin getting it up and running.

You're going to need some practical skills and the right equipment and tools. You will be equipped with the skills you have to jumpstart your own dropshipping company by the time you've done it.

9. Dropshipping grow easily.

Your business model doesn't even have to alter that much at all when you scale up. As you expand, you'll have to bring more effort into sales and marketing, but your daily life will remain almost the same.

One of the advantages of dropshipping is that when you scale, the costs do not spike. It's convenient to keep rising at a fairly high pace because of this. If you choose to build a little team at any stage, you can manage about anything by yourself, too.

10. Dropshipping doesn't need a big capital.

Since you need very little to start a dropshipping business, you can get underway with minimal funds. Right from your desktop, you can create a whole corporation, and you do not need to make any heavy investment. Your costs would be reasonably low even as your company grows, particularly compared to normal business expenses.

11. Dropshipping is flexible.

This is one of the greatest advantages. You get to be a boss of your own and set your own regulations. It's one of the most versatile occupations anyone can try.

With just a laptop, you can operate from anywhere, and you can operate at the hours that are most comfortable for you. For founders that want a company that fits for them, this is perfect. To get stuff done, you won't have to lean over backward. You choose your own pace instead.

Dropshipping is indeed flexible in that it allows you plenty of space to create choices that fit for you. Whenever you choose, you can quickly list new items, and you can change your plans on the move. You should automate it to work when you're gone, whether you're going on holiday. You get the concept prospects are limitless.

12. Dropshipping manages easily.

Because it doesn't need you to make several commitments, with no hassle, you can manage everything. When you have found and set up suppliers, you are often exclusively liable for your e-commerce store.

Chapter 2. How Dropshipping Works

Dropshipping functions by third-party suppliers, which deliver goods for each order on a just-in-time basis. When a sales order is received by the retailer, they transfer the requirements to the supplier—who manufactures the product.

While dropshipping is used by many e-commerce retailers as the base of their business processes, dropshipping can be used successfully to complement traditional retail inventory-stocking models. Because dropshipping does not create any unused surplus inventory, it may be used for analysis purposes before committing to sale on a marketplace, such as testing the waters.

Dropshipping works because, with the aid of a third party such as a wholesaler or an e-commerce shop, a dropshipper fulfills orders to deliver the goods for an even cheaper price. The majority of dropshippers offer goods directly from Chinese suppliers because the prices of most products in China are very poor. If the wholesaler's price is 5 dollars for a product. A dropshipper sells it for $8 and retains $3 for himself. The bulk of dropshippers target nations with higher purchasing power.

2.1 Awareness about the Supply Chain

You'll see the word "supply chain" a lot in here. It seems like a fancy lingo for the business, but it actually applies to how a product transfers from seller to consumer. We'll use this to explain the method of dropshipping.

2.2 The Supply Chain Process

You, the merchant, are only one puzzle piece. An effective dropshipping mechanism depends on several parties all acting in sync together. The supply chain is just that: producer, supplier, and retailer coordination.

You should split down the supply chain into three simple steps:

- The producer manufactures the goods and supplies them to wholesalers & retailers.

Let's say maker A is manufacturing bottles of water. They are marketed in bulk to manufacturers and wholesalers after the bottles come off the assembly line, who switch around & resell the bottles to dealers.

- Suppliers and wholesalers market the products to dealers.

For a particular type of product, a retailer like yourself is searching for a supplier. An arrangement to operate together is then reached between the retailer and the supplier.

A little point here: Although you may order directly from product producers, purchasing from retailers is always much cheaper instead. There are minimum purchasing criteria for most suppliers that can be very high, and you will still have to purchase stock & ship the goods.

So, purchasing directly from the producer might seem quicker, but you would profit more from buying from distributors (dealing with the little profit).

Suppliers are often convenient since all of them are skilled in a specific niche, so the type of items you need can be quickly identified. This also implies that you'll get started to sell super quick.

- Retailers sell goods to buyers.

Suppliers & wholesalers should not market to the public directly; that's the task of the retailer. The last move between the product & the consumer is the supplier.

Online stores from which customers buy goods are provided by retailers. The merchant marks it up again to reach at the final price after the wholesaler rates up the items. By "markup," we apply to fixing a premium that covers the product's cost price and gives you a benefit.

It's that! From start to end, it is the whole supply chain. In business, it's a simple but crucial concept.

You may have noted that no other group has been alluded to as a dropshipper. That is because there is no particular function for "dropshipper." Dropshipping is actually the activity of somebody else delivering goods. Technically, producers, retailers, and merchants will all be dropshippers.

Later on, we'll discuss how to start a retail dropshipping company in this guide. In other terms, you can learn how to become a trader who buys commodities from wholesalers to market to the public. This may indicate that through an online storefront, you sell through eBay or even your own website.

Remember what it's like for the consumer now that you realize what the supply chain is like.

2.3 What is Fulfillment?

Order fulfillment that's all the steps a corporation requires in having a fresh order and bringing the order into the hands of the customer. The procedure includes storing, picking & packaging the products, distributing them and sending the consumer an automatic email to let them know that the product is in transit.

2.4 The Steps to make Order Fulfillment

There are some steps involved in order fulfillment, which are as under:-

1. Receiving inventory.

Essentially, there are two approaches for an eCommerce company to manage inventory. It can decide to receive & stock the in-house inventory, or it can employ an outsourcer for eCommerce order fulfillment to take control of the inventory and other associated activities. The organization would be liable for taking stock, inspecting the product, marking, and maintaining the inventory method if it opts for the first alternative. If the business wishes to outsource or dropships, the order fulfillment agent or supplier can perform certain duties.

2. Storing inventory.

If you plan to stock the inventory yourself, after the receiving portion is finished, there'll be another list of assignments waiting for you. Shelving the inventory and holding a careful watch on what goods come in and what goods are going out would be the key activities on the list so that you can deliver the orders without any complications.

3. Processing the order.

Businesses who outsource order fulfillment do not have to get through the nitty-gritty of order delivery since they actually move on to their partner's order request and let them manage the rest. This is the phase where the order is taken off the shelves, shipped to a packaging station, examined for any damage, packed and transferred to the shipping station for businesses who handle their own product.

4. Shipping the order.

The best delivery strategy is calculated based on the scale, weight and precise specifications of the order. A third-party contractor is typically contracted to complete this phase.

Returns Handling. For online shoppers, the opportunity to refund unwanted goods quickly is a big factor in the purchase phase. You ought to design a crystal straightforward return policy that is readily available to all the customers and workers to ensure the receipt, repair and redemption of the returned goods are as successful as practicable. It will help you prevent needless confusion and errors by making this step automated.

Chapter 3. Why dropshipping is one of the best way to make money in 2021.

According to Forrester (analyst) Reports, the magnitude of online retail revenues would be $370 billion by the end of 2017. In comparison, 23 percent, which amounts to $85.1 billion, would come from dropshipping firms. To many businesses, like startups, this sheer scale alone is attractive.

An online retailer following this concept appears similar to its traditional e-commerce competitors by appearance. Dropshipping may be a well-kept mystery in the e-commerce world as consumers just think about the goods, price and credibility of the shop rather than how the goods are sourced and who delivers the shipments.

In summary,' dropshipping' is a business strategy in which the supplier does not directly hold the inventory or process the orders in his or her control. Both orders are delivered directly from a wholesaler and delivered. This encourages the supplier to concentrate on the business's selling aspect.

Many major e-commerce names, such as Zappos, began with dropshipping. For those that seek motivation, billion-dollar dropshipping internet store Wayfair or the milliondollarBlinds.com are top examples today.

Five explanations of how the dropshipping business strategy appeals to both startups and experienced entrepreneurs are offered below. These issues in traditional e-commerce have been nagging challenges, which can be addressed with the dropshipping model immediately.

3.1 Dropshipping Is The E-Commerce Future

It seem that dropshipping will be the future of e-commerce. Here are some main reasons which explain this concept.

Sourcing of Product:

Conventional e-commerce stores must directly import supplies from wholesalers, frequently based in various countries. They often need goods to be bought in bulk and are then shipped prior to being promoted and distributed to the local warehouse. A lot of time, money & resources are required for the whole phase. The presence of expensive intermediaries, such as banks, freight shipments and export-import brokers, also involves it.

The dropshipping model, however, enables manufacturers to market goods for large quantities of each product without needing to think about sourcing. The entire method is substantially simplified with just a turn-key e-commerce storefront such as Shopify and a dropshipping software like Oberlo. The retailer may choose to notify the distributors via e-mail to tell them that their supplies are now being shipped to the store. The most of the procedure can be quickly handled from the dashboard, such as uploading product images, updating pricing and order monitoring.

Storage

A traditional e-commerce store, particularly as it carries multiple or large products, requires large storage spaces. It might be imaginable to store ten to 100 items, but storing 1,000 or 1,000,000 items will cost a real fortune that is not within the reach of a start-up. This high warehouse rent issue is addressed by the dropshipping model since the goods remain with the distributor or wholesale retailer until they are bought.

Order fulfillment

Many pioneers of e-commerce do not foresee investing most of their time picking, packaging and delivering orders. They should, of course, outsource the order fulfillment for ease to a boutique e-commerce fulfillment, such as ShipMonk. The dropshipping model, however, facilitates hands-free shipment, since the whole packaging and shipping process is in the possession of the wholesaler or distributor.

Cataloging & photography

A conventional e-commerce shop owner has to take professional-quality images of items that may be very pricey, like a decent digital camera, a light panel, lighting and some more. For a dropshipping control software, this issue is fixed, as the "product importing" function allows for instant picture import.

Scalability

Wayfair.com is a major online dropshipping store that holds 10,000 vendors of more than eight million items. Yes, $8 million. By this business model, such huge scalability is made possible.

Because the retailer just has to work on the publicity and customer care aspect, they don't have to think about the warehouse's rent and other operating expenses skyrocketing.

In conclusion, the dropshipping paradigm offers the ability for tiny startups with minimal capital to contend with large and medium online stores comfortably, rendering the field of e-commerce an equal environment for everyone. That being said, plan in the future to see more e-commerce shops adopting this model.

Chapter 4. Niche And Product Selection

You want a business to start, but the thing that holds you down is the market niche that you feel you need to pick. And, honestly, it can be tricky: you might mention all your interests & passions and yet feel like you haven't hit the singular thing that you were expected to do.

Yet, it can trigger paralysis to place some sort of burden on yourself to choose the very right niche.

Certainly, in choosing a suitable niche business, you like to do your careful research, but it's easier to get up and run than to wait around. You will try ideas that way, enter the market earlier, and benefit from the victories and losses. That way, too, you can still take what you have gained from previous attempts, so step on with fresh concepts if the first company does not take off.

4.1 Steps how to search your right niche

Using the following five methods to find your niche, whether you're unable to determine or you need more information to work with.

1. Identify your interests & passions.

This could be something that you have achieved before. But, if you haven't, quickly make a compilation of 10 topical passions and areas of passion.

Business isn't easy, and it can challenge you at any stage. If you work in an area you don't care for, the likelihood of leaving will increase significantly — especially like a first sole proprietor.

This doesn't mean that a better match has to be found. You can stay with it if you are excited about any part of running the business. If you don't care about the issue, you might not be able to easily find the drive to persevere within.

2. Identify problems that you can solve.

You're able to get to narrow down your choices with your list of ten topics in hand. You first need to identify challenges that your target clients are facing to build a viable enterprise, then decide if you can potentially fix them. Here are a few items you should do to find issues in different niches.

3. Research your competition.

There is not always a bad thing in the presence of competition. It can actually show you that you've discovered a market that's lucrative. Although you do have to do an in-depth analysis of competing pages.

Build a fresh spreadsheet and start tracking all the competing websites that you can find.

And find out whether there's already an opening in the crowd to stick out. Are you still willing to rate the keywords? Is there really a way to distinguish and build a unique offer for yourself? Here are some indications that you will enter a niche and flourish, even though it is already covered by other sites:

- Content of poor quality. In a niche where several company owners are not delivering high-quality, informative content that suits the viewer, it's easy to outrank the competitors.
- Lack of transparency. By establishing an authentic and accessible identity in a niche where most platforms are faceless and unnecessarily corporate, many internet marketers have disrupted whole industries.
- The lack of paid competitiveness. If you have noticed a keyword with a relatively high search rate but little competition with paying ads, there is undoubtedly a potential for you to upset the business.

4. Determine the profitability of the niche.

You need to have a fairly decent understanding now about what niche you're about to get into. You might not have limited your selection down to a particular region of the topic, but you've certainly noticed a few suggestions that you feel pretty good about. It's important to have an idea at this stage about how much money you have the opportunity to make in your niche. A fine way to go to continue your search is ClickBank.

So, browse the category's best brands. That is not a positive indication if you can't locate any offers. It could mean that the niche could not be monetized by someone.

You're in luck if the quest throws up a good amount of products — just not an excessive amount of products. Take notice of pricing points such that your own goods can be marketed in a fair way.

Bear in mind, though, that you may not have to launch your organization with your own product offering. You should collaborate in your niche with product makers, marketers and site owners to start earning commissions when working on your innovative solution.

5. Test your idea.

You are now prepared with all the knowledge you need to pick a niche, and checking your proposal is the only thing needed to do. Setting up a landing page for pre-sales of a product you're producing is one easy way to do this. Through paying ads, you will then push traffic to this page.

That doesn't actually mean that you are not in a viable niche, even though you don't get pre-sales. Your message may not be quite correct, or you haven't found the right deal yet. You will maximize conversions by using A/B split testing to figure out whether there is something preventing the target group from taking action or not.

You will sell to two fundamental markets: customer and corporation. Such divisions are reasonably clear. "For example, if you sell women's clothes from a department shop, shoppers are your target market; if you sell office supplies, companies are your target market (this is referred to as "B2B" sales). In certain instances, for example, you could be selling to both corporations and people if you operate a printing company.

No company, especially a small one, can be everything to all individuals. The more you can describe your target group broadly, the stronger. For even the larger corporations, this method is recognized as building a market and is crucial to growth. Walmart and Tiffany are also stores, but they have somewhat different niches: Walmart caters to bargain-minded customers, while Tiffany tends to luxury jewelry buyers.

"Some entrepreneurs make the error of slipping into the "all over the map" pit instead of building a niche, believing they can do many things and be successful at all of them. Falkenstein warns that these individuals soon learn a difficult lesson: "Smaller is larger in market, and smaller is not across the map; it is extremely focused."

4.2 Creating a good niche

Keep in mind these important to create a good niche:

1. Make a wish list.

Who do you like to do business with? Be as descriptive as you are capable of. Identify the regional spectrum and the kinds of firms or clients that you want your organization to target. You can't make contact if you do not really know whom you are going to do business with. Falkenstein cautions, "You must recognize that you can't do business with everyone." Otherwise, you risk leaving yourself exhausted and confusing your buyers.

The trend is toward small niches these days. It's not precise enough to target teens; targeting adult, African American teenagers with the family incomes of $40,000 or more is. It is too large to target corporations that market apps; it is a better aim to target Northern California-based firms that offer internet software distribution and training that have sales of $15 million or more.

2. Focus.

Clarify what you intend to sell, knowing that a) to all customers, you can't be all items and b) smaller is better. Your specialty isn't the same as that of sector you are employed in. A retail apparel corporation, for example, is not a niche but a sector. Maternity clothes for corporate mothers" may be a more specific niche."

Using these strategies to assist you in starting this focus process:

- Create a compilation of the greatest activities you do and the talents that are inherent in many of them.
- List your accomplishments.
- Identify the important things of life that you've experienced.
- Look for trends that reflect your personality or approach to addressing issues.

Your niche should emerge from your desires and expertise in a normal way. For instance, if you spent 10 years of working in such a consulting firm and also ten years working for such a small, family-owned company, you may actually have to start a consulting company that specializes in limited, family-owned businesses.

3. Describe the customer's worldview.

A good corporation utilizes what Falkenstein called the Platinum Rule: "Do to the others as they're doing to themselves." You will define their desires or desires as you look at the situation from the viewpoint of your prospective clients. Talking to new clients and recognizing their biggest issues is the perfect approach to achieve this.

4. Synthesize.

Your niche can begin to take shape at this point when the opinions and the desires of the consumer and desire to coalesce to create something different. There are five attributes of a Strong Niche:

- In other terms, it relates to your long-term view and carries you where you like to go.
- Somebody else needs it, consumers in particular.
- It is closely arranged.
- It's one-of-a-kind, "the only city game."
- It evolves, enabling you to build multiple profit centers and yet maintain the core market, thus guaranteeing long-term success.

5. Evaluate.

It is now time to test the product or service proposed against the five requirements in Phase 4. Perhaps you'll notice that more business travel than that you're ready for is needed for niche you had in mind. That indicates that one of the above conditions is not met-it will not carry you where you like to go. Scrap it, and pass on to the next proposal.

6. Test.

Test-market it until you have a balance between the niche and the product. "Give individuals an opportunity to purchase your product or service, not just theoretically, but actually put it out there." By giving samples, such as a complimentary mini-seminar or a preview copy of the newsletter, this can be accomplished. "If you spend enormous sums of cash on the initial trial run, you're possibly doing it wrong," she says. The research shouldn't cost you a bunch of money:

7. Go for it!

It is time for your idea to be implemented. This is the most challenging step for many entrepreneurs. But worry not: if you have done your research, it would be a measured risk to reach the business, not simply a chance.

Chapter 5. How to start dropshipping business in 2021

It's not easy to learn the way to start a dropshipping company, as with any type of business. Nevertheless, it's a perfect first move in the world of business. Without keeping any inventory, you may sell to customers. You do not have to pay upfront for goods. And if you are passionate about your new venture, in the long term, you will create a sustainable source of revenue.

In this complete dropshipping guide, suggest taking the following market and financial moves if you are considering dropshipping.

Others are mandatory from the start, and others are only a smart idea, so it will save you time and stress down the line by coping with them up front.

Dropshipping is a method of order fulfillment that helps shop owners to deliver without stocking any stock directly to buyers. If a consumer orders a commodity from a dropshipping shop, it is delivered directly to them by a third-party retailer. The client pays the selling price that you set, you pay the market price of the vendors, and the rest is benefit. You never need to maintain goods or spend in inventory.

You are responsible for designing a website and your own label, as well as selecting and promoting the items you choose to offer in the dropshipping business strategy. Your corporation is therefore liable for the expense of shipping and for setting rates that result in a reasonable profit margin.

Steps For Starting A Dropshipping Profitable Business

Learn to find high-margin products, introduce them to your business, and easily begin selling them.

1. Commit yourself for starting a dropshipping business

Dropshipping, as in any other business, needs considerable effort and a long-term focus. You're going to be deeply surprised if you're looking for a six-figure benefit from 6 weeks of part-time employment. You would be far less likely to get frustrated and leave by entering the organization with reasonable assumptions regarding the commitment needed and the prospects for benefit.

You'll need to spend heavily when beginning a dropshipping venture, utilizing one of the two following currencies: time or funds.

Investing time in dropshipping business

Our recommended strategy, particularly for the first dropshipping developers, is bootstrapping & investing sweat equity to develop your company. For various factors, we prefer this method over spending a huge amount of money:

- You will understand how the organization works inside out, which, as the enterprise expands and scales, will be crucial for handling others.
- You would know your clients and business personally, helping you to make smarter choices.
- You would be less inclined to waste huge amounts on vanity ventures that are not vital to success.
- You will build some new talents that will enable you a stronger entrepreneur.

Realistically, most persons are not ready to leave their work in order to ramp up their own online shop for six months. It might be a little more complicated, but even though you're already doing a 9-to-5 job, it's surely feasible to get underway with dropshipping, assuming you set reasonable standards for your customers about customer support and delivery times. When you continue to expand, as much as working capital and profitability allow, you will move into working long hours on your company.

Both companies and entrepreneurs are specific, but it is feasible to produce a monthly income stream of $1,000-$2,000 within 12 months of working around 10 to 15 hours per week to develop the firm.

Excited regarding starting a new business but not knowing where to begin? This informative guide will show you how to identify great products with strong sales potential that are newly trendy.

If you have the choice of working long hours on your company, that's the best option to increase your profit prospects and the possibility of good dropshipping. It is particularly beneficial in the early days to concentrate all the energies on publicity when creating traction is essential. It would normally take approximately 12 months of full-time jobs based on our knowledge, with a heavy focus on publicity for a dropshipping firm to replace an annual full-time salary of $50,000.

For a very small payout, it might sound like a lot of work, but bear these two points in mind:

When the dropshipping company is up and going, it would actually require considerably less time than from a 40-hour-per-week work to maintain it. In terms of the reliability and scalability that the dropshipping paradigm offers, much of your expenditure pays off.

You establish more than just a revenue stream when you develop a company. You also build an asset that you will market in the future. Be sure that when looking at the true return, you remember the equity valuation you are accruing, and also the cash flow produced.

Investing money in dropshipping business

By spending a lot of capital, it is feasible to develop and grow a dropshipping company, but we suggest against it. We attempted all methods to growing an enterprise (bootstrapping it ourselves vs. outsourcing the procedure), and while we were in the trenches doing much of the work, we had the most progress.

In the early stages, it is vital to have someone who is profoundly involved in the company's future to construct it from the ground up. You would be at the hands of pricey engineers, developers, and advertisers who will easily eat away whatever money you produce without knowing how your organization operates at any stage. You don't have to do everything it yourself, but at the start of your company, we highly advocate becoming the primary motivating power.

To have your company started and operating, you would, though, require a modest cash reserve in the $1,000 range. For limited administrative costs (like web hosting and dropshipping providers), you may need this and to pay some incorporation fees, which we will cover below.

2. Dropshipping business idea to chose

The second phase in studying how to launch a dropshipping company is to do the market research required. You want to find a niche you are interested in and make choices based on how effective it can be, almost like though you were starting a grocery shop and checking at the numerous sites, rivals, and developments. But the fact is, it's tricky to come up with product concepts to offer.

Niche goods also have a more passionate client base, which, through increasing awareness about the items, will make marketing to unique audiences simpler. A good entry point to begin dropshipping without cash could be health, clothes, makeup goods, appliances, phone accessories, or yoga-related pieces.

Any instances of dropshipping stores in a niche may be:

- Dog bow and ties for dog lovers
- Exercise equipment for fitness
- iPhone cases and cables for iPhone owners
- Camping gear for campers

To try the dropshipping business ideas, you may also use the appropriate techniques:

Google Trends could really help you identify whether, as well as the seasons in which they tend to trend, a product is trending up or down. Notice the search volume is not indicated by Google Patterns. But if you're using it, be sure to use a keyword tool such as Keywords Everywhere to cross-check your data to determine the popularity of the product in search.

3. Do competitor research

You want to check about your competitors so that you know what you're trying to sell in your shop and appreciate the way they operate. Your competitors may have great success hints which can help you develop a better marketing strategy for your dropshipping firm.

Limit your study to only five other dropshipping firms, like one or two major players such as Walmart or Ebay, if your business has a number of competitors (that is a positive thing in dropshipping). It will help you remain centered and prepare your next phase.

4. Choose a dropshipping supplier

Choosing a supplier for dropshipping is a crucial move towards creating a profitable dropshipping business. A dropshipping company does not have any goods to ship to consumers without vendors and would thus cease to operate.

At this stage, you analyzed what goods you want to offer and realize that they can be profitable, and you want to know where to find a provider of dropshipping that provides you with the high-quality service that you need to grow. By linking Oberlo to the online store, eCommerce platforms such as Shopify provide a plug-and-play style alternative to find possible suppliers.

5. Build your ecommerce store

An eCommerce platform such as Shopify is the next what you need to launch a dropshipping business. This is the home where you deliver traffic, offer goods, and payments are processed.

These type of platforms makes the e-commerce website simple to create and launch. It is a complete commerce service that connects you to sell and receive payments in several ways, like online, sell in different currencies, and conveniently manage products.

To use e-commerce websites, you don't need to become a programmer or developer either. They have resources to assist with anything from domain name ideas to logo design, and with the store creator and Payment processing themes, you are quickly able to modify the feel and look of your store.

6. Market your dropshipping store

It's time to talk about promoting your new shop, now that you know to start a dropshipping firm. You may want to bring more work into your marketing and promotional activities while developing the dropshipping business strategy to stick out in your market.

You will invest time working on selling and supporting the company in the following ways, with too many stuff about dropshipping being processed:

- Paid ads (Facebook & Google).

For a Facebook ad, the average cost is about 0.97 cents per click, that's not too bad if you're new to social media advertising. Facebook ads are extensible, goods can perform ok on them, and they click into the desire of people to purchase momentum. You can run Google Shopping Ads and target lengthy keywords that are more likely to be purchased by shoppers. Typically, with Google ads, there is more price competition, but it might be worthy of your time to check it out.

- Influencer marketing.

You may have a low funds for marketing your business as a new dropshipper. Influencer marketing is also an affordable way to target audience because individuals are more likely than traditional advertising to trust influencers. When you go this route, start negotiating an affiliate fee versus a flat rate with the influencer. It's a win-win situation, as every sale they're going to make money off, and the cost is going to be less for you.

- Mobile marketing.

Smartphone marketing is a broad term referring to a company that connects with clients on their mobile phones. You can start with a VIP text club, for example, and encourage website users to sign up for the exclusive promotions & deals. Or provide client support through Messenger in a live chat session with shoppers. You can create automated qualified leads, customer loyalty, and cart abandonment campaigns with a mobile marketing tool such as ManyChat to drive sales and profits for your dropshipping business.

Stay updated on what channels are operating and which are not, as with any profitable online business, especially if you invest money in them like paid ads. You can always adjust your marketing plan to lower costs as well as maximize revenue as you keep growing and improve your business.

7. Analyze your offering

You should start looking at the consequences of your diligent work after you've been promoting and operating your dropshipping company for some time. Any analytics will help you address some critical online shop queries, like:

* Sales

What are my channels with the highest performance? Where am I expected to put more ad dollars? What else are my favorite items for sale? What are my greatest clients?

* Behavior of shoppers

Do citizens buy more on their laptops or cell phones? For each unit, what's the conversion rate?

- Margins of profit

Why are the most profitable pieces and variant SKUs? What do my month-over-month revenue and gross income look like?

To track web traffic over time and optimize your search engine optimization activities, you can even use resources like Google Analytics & Search Console. Plus, you review the results monthly to guarantee that your overall plan succeeds with your business, whether you are utilizing third-party software for your social network or messenger marketing.

You want to build a data-informed analytics framework while building a dropshipping e-commerce store. Remain compatible with what you evaluate over time and calculate the consistency of your store against simple KPIs. This will encourage you to make better choices for your store, so move your small business over time to the next level.

Chapter 6. How To identify Best Suppliers For Your New Dropshipping Business

Dropshipping is a model for eCommerce that is increasingly attractive. That is because launching a dropshipping company is simpler (not to say less expensive) than managing inventory for a traditional digital storefront.

The whole model of drop shipment is focused on the retailer doing its job well and delivering orders timely and effectively. It goes without saying, therefore, that identifying the appropriate supplier is one, if not the most important, and a step towards creating a successful brand. If an order is messed up by your supplier/seller, you and your organization are liable, so the trick is to find someone who adheres to the schedule and is open to discuss any problems

The advantages and disadvantages of dropshipping are well known, but it has become far less obvious that the most significant part of beginning a dropshipping business is choosing the right vendors for your WooCommerce shop. Until now.

6.1 The Importance of Selecting The Right Suppliers

A special model for eCommerce is Dropshipping. To retain their own inventories, conventional online retailers compensate. Those expenses are all but offset by dropshipping, so dropshipping would not need substantial start-up investment.

In the other side, dropshipping suggests that you place the destiny of your eCommerce store in the possession of others.

With the dropshipping system, retailers focus on wholesalers, manufacturers, and dealers who meet the orders of the retailers.

The dropshipping puzzle has several parts, and for the greater image, each component is critical. Among those pieces, one of the most significant is dropshipping suppliers. In reality, the finest dropshippers know that a dropshipping eCommerce store can make or break the efficiency and overall reliability of dropshipping suppliers.

6.2 Finding Your Dropshipping Suppliers

It needs you to partner with manufacturers, wholesalers, & distributors to start a dropshipping business. You want to identify vendors who improve the dropshipping business rather than compromise it.

Research Your Products

You have to figure out what types of things you can sell before you can start finding and working with vendors.

You want to address queries in specific, such as:

- Where does the item come from?
- How long would manufacturing take?
- How is it done?

Are there factors of height or weight which might make fulfillment more complicated or more costly?

The purpose is not expertise; however, you want to get to know the goods so that you can help determine which ones are suitable for dropshipping.

Understand the supply chain and recognize the considerations

You need to get familiar with dropship supply chain after nailing down your goods. In other terms, you should to know how it works for dropshipping.

For dropshipping, the items never really go into the hands of the dealer. Instead, an order is issued by the retailer, and a supplier who manages packing and delivery initiates fulfillment. In this way, the dealer is like the director of a dropshipping company.

You can't sell goods if you don't have reputable vendors, which suggests that you don't have a dropshipping business.

You need to get familiar with dropship supply chain since nailing down your products. In other terms, you need to understand how it functions for dropshipping.

For dropshipping, the items never really go into the hands of the dealer. Instead, an order is issued by the retailer and a supplier who manages packing and delivery initiates fulfilment. In this manner, the retailer is just like the director of a dropshipping company.

You can't sell goods if you don't have reputable suppliers, which suggests that you don't have a dropshipping business.

Search for Dropshipping Wholesalers on Google

You will identify the major vendors for your preferred commodities or product types with a Google search.

When you build a preliminary list, by studying the next few queries, take notice of the various characteristics of dropshipping suppliers.

- What is supplier location?
- Will the retailer link with your WooCommerce shop so that fresh orders are immediately submitted for fulfillment?
- What (if any) is the sum of minimum order (MOQ)?
- What support (e.g., mobile, email, chat, etc.) does the provider offer?
- What kind of range of items does the retailer offer?

Subscribe to Dropshipping Suppliers Directories

And if lots of choices pop up in the Google searches, directories will bring even more options. For a broad selection of items, these repositories comprise of web lists of dropshipping vendors and wholesalers.

You should recognize that some of the finest are premium directories, such as Salehoo and Worldwide Labels, implying they need paying subscriptions. There are a lot of free directories accessible that you can access at no fee, like Wholesale Central. Free directories, though, are occasionally obsolete. Newer vendors do not exist, and suppliers are also listed who are no longer in operation.

Usually, premium directories vary in cost from $20 a month for lifetime access to a few hundred bucks. You can find the expense of a premium directory to be beneficial, with free directories often hit-or-miss. There are also premium directories, like Doba, explicitly customized for dropshipping.

Figure Out Your Competitor's Suppliers

It follows that you must see what your competitors do if you want to be successful in the dropshipping field. Do any acknowledgment, in fact, to see which manufacturers are meeting their requirements.

There are a lot of methods to do this, but testing the markets that the competitors sell is the best.

If the supplier is not listed on the page, by making your own order, you will always show the supplier. Since the retailer is pleased, an invoice or packaging slip from them would possibly be included with the shipment. To ask about a partnership with your own dropshipping company, you can then contact the supplier directly.

Attend Trade Seminars

Trade shows have been considered to be an efficient place for manufacturers to set up and grow their companies. So, if you haven't been to a trade seminar yet, add it to the end of the list of to-do events.

You network with other participants within dropship supply chain, like distributors and dropshipping wholesalers, at trade shows. You get an insider's view on current and future products that you should introduce to your online store. For dropshipping businesses, you even get to "talk shop" face-to-face, which is also the most successful way to do business.

Join Industry Groups and Networks

Trade shows facilitate with locating vendors for dropshipping firms, yet another effective resource is business networks and groups.

The majority of retailers, like the identities of their dropshipping vendors, are not willing to share the secrets of their performance. The individuals who enter business groups, however, want to share, learn, & develop. Through being part of the dropshipping network, you will get valuable insight from industry professionals. Your colleagues, for instance, might recommend better suppliers or alert you about suppliers in order to avoid.

Connect with the Manufacturers

Not all manufacturers supply to consumers directly, although there are those who do. Until picking vendors for your eCommerce dropshipping shop, suggest reaching out to the producers of the goods that you will market.

You have far higher margins when a producer chooses to be the distributor than with a traditional retailer or wholesaler. Manufacturers, on the other hand, frequently impose minimum order amounts that could need bigger orders. You might find yourself with considerable inventory to deal in this situation, which is intended to circumvent dropshipping.

Ask the vendor to recommend vendors for you if a manufacturer won't work with you. A recommendation, after all, indicates that the agreements and commitments between a manufacturer and a supplier is successful. For that cause, it is definitely worth putting suggested vendors on your list of possibilities.

Order Samples

There's no substitution for firsthand knowledge, no matter how many feedback or testimonials you find. This is why ordering samples is the next phase in finding the correct dropshipping suppliers for the business.

Ordering samples teaches you a few key things about a supplier. First one is that you get to know the product's consistency yourself.

The second is that you will see how delivery is done by the retailer, and what shipment packaging seems to if a different vendor is involved, and how long it takes to ship and distribute. Suppliers will execute the requests, so buying samples provides you with an idea of what your clients will feel.

Confirm Contract Terms & Fees

You compiled several options, removed any but the most suitable possibilities, ordered tests to assess certain vendors, and decided on your dropshipping company with the right supplier (or suppliers). Negotiating deal conditions and payments is the last option left to do.

New businesses with unproven consumer bases have fewer bargaining leverage relative to mature companies with established customer bases. When it comes to communicating the margins, this is especially true.

Since dropshipping means that you don't have to hold your inventory, there would be low margins. The bulk of inventory costs and expenditures involved with meeting your orders is borne by your supplier(s). With dropshipping, because prices are smaller, gross margins are often lower than if you stored and delivered orders personally.

With margins generally poor, the fees concerned may be the biggest distinction between vendors. Such suppliers, for instance, charge flat per-order rates that are applied to the overall cost of the goods. Per-order payments typically vary from $2 and $5 to cover delivery and shipping costs (although big or unwieldy goods can require higher fees).

In the end, you want to select the supplier(s) that satisfies your specifications and give contracts of appropriate terms.

Chapter 7. Setting Up Your Dropshipping business On A Budget

The establishment of a dropshipping company as an eCommerce business is a perfect way to earn money. Managing a business without the hassle of product and shipping logistics is the most convincing aspect of a dropshipping store

You have already heard stories from businessmen about how costly it is to start a business. This involve accounts of hopelessly pursuing buyers or firms failing because of bleak financials to remain afloat. Do not let this scare you from launching a dropshipping store, as this model enables you to offer low-risk products.

What you need to do is get the orders and call the supplier-the rest is up to them.

There are very few financial barriers associated with the establishment of a dropshipping store when it comes to financing the company. In fact, with around zero initial investment, you can get underway with an online store.

Here's a 7-step feasible plan for launching a dropshipping shop on a budget shoestring.

1. Research Your Options

You'll need to do some research before beginning some form of business.

It requires getting online and finding out the competitors that offer related goods. To see just what each has to suggest, you'll also want to spend a little time investigating the future vendors and distributors.

Each shipping group will have a specific way of doing stuff and pricing models, therefore pay careful attention to those specifics so that you can ensure that you team up with your dropshipping store with the right party.

2. Create a Plan to Stick

You'll need to get a solid plan in progress before you can launch your business activities. A budget is used with this. It's important to decide what your budget is, whether you have $100 or $500 to get underway and ensure that you adhere to it. The easiest way to achieve so is to maintain good track of all your spending to guarantee that as you start up your store, you do not go over the budget.

3. Find Your Niche

In reality, many believe that it is an impossible task. It may be really challenging to appeal to all. Instead, rather than attempting to market could product under the sun, choose the goods focused on a particular niche.

Select a particular area of the business, such as organic pet food or dog clothes, if you decide that you want to market animal-related items.

When you can refine your attention down, you can have a much higher sales rate, and you are more likely to be noticed when customers are looking for a particular form of a product. Your small shop can get lost in the noise of competitors if your focus is too big.

4. Set Up Your eCommerce website

This is the phase through which you finally launch and set up your site with a dropshipping store.

Three of the most successful eCommerce sites accessible to sellers today are Shopify and Wix. It's quick to get started, as well as its user-friendly interface, also for sellers who are not especially tech-savvy, makes configuration and maintenance easy.

With monthly prices of less than $40, Shopify and Wix are both inexpensive alternatives, making it a perfect way to get off on a budget in the digital marketplace. You may also open a Modalyst store to boost the delivery and streamline the distribution process.

You're able to move on to the next stage after you have set up a simple online storefront that has your products selected.

5. Make Meetings With Your Suppliers

When it comes to choosing which provider to use it for your dropshipping shop, there are lots of decisions out there. Because you've done your homework in phase one already, now is the moment where your decision is formalized. Through entering into a contract with the commodity distributor(s) of your choosing, you will do so. Any of the most successful shipping partners makes it simple to get started, and in no time, unlike having to pay such upfront costs, you will be on your way.

The most relevant issues you are asking your prospective suppliers are:

- Do you keep all products in stock?
- How do you care the returns?
- What is your normal or average processing time?
- In which areas do you ship to? Do international shipping available?
- What kind of support did you offer?
- Is there any limit for orders?

You would have a solid understanding about how your suppliers conduct their company until you meet a supplier who addresses certain questions to your satisfaction. In addition, as a seller dealing for them, you'll realize what you need to do. You're on the path to a successful working partnership at this point.

6. Start Selling

Oh, congratulations. In launching your online store, this is one of most exciting steps. It's time to add your product details to your website and start selling until you have all your arrangements and agreements in order.

If customers are not aware of the products, you will not have enough sales, to begin with. You'll want to waste more time and money on ads if this is the case. By beginning with low-cost advertisements on Instagram and Facebook, or advertising on blogs as well as other websites which have a common audience, you will keep advertising costs reasonably small.

7. Optimize Your Site

You should take some time to customize the website until you have some revenue and knowledge under your belt. You can do all this earlier in the process, but waiting to see what is really working before you start to make changes is often a good idea.

There are a broad variety of customization choices for sites such as Shopify and Modalyst, including templates that change the way your website looks and plugins to can customize how your website works. The primary aim here is to tweak the site in ways that make it smoother for your clients and more organized.

As you've seen, all it takes to set up an online store is a few steps, and most of them don't need any money. You're not lonely if you're excited about being an owner of an eCommerce company just don't have a ton of money to launch with. This is why so many platforms are accessible that make it easier to get started without investing a million in the process.

Making sure that it works and prepare a strategy that you will use to guide you when keeping under your budget by setting up your dropshipping business, no matter how small it might be.

Chapter 8. Mistakes To Avoid When Developing Your Dropshipping Business

In an environment that jumps at the chance to make a business deal quick and convenient, Dropshipping tends to have a no for retailers. It might seem like, now, acquiring the goods and marketing with a bit of savvy are your only worries. Yet, if you wish to hold the company afloat, you should not forget about the client's perspective. True, the boring duties of inventory, order filling, and then ensuring shipping can be passed on.

The dropshipping company, however, does not waste any time thinking about the feelings of your client. How do you assume if your client is going to be satisfied? The buyers are the ones who put the money back. Anything falls out the window if they're not satisfied. You would need to consider the duties and what failures typically trigger it all to backfire in order to completely enjoy the advantages of utilizing dropshipping.

Here are a common mistake that leads to the failure end of your dropshipping business, so you should hold these mistakes in mind all the time.

1. Worrying About Shipping Costs.

While shipping costs might be a doozy, it's never productive to stress. In this area, you will need to decide under which your priorities lie. Shipping prices can vary all over the board, depending on where orders come from. This stress can be relieved by setting a flat rate and generally evens out with time. Not only does this make things easier for you, but it's also simple and easy for customers.

2. Relying Much on Vendors.

By putting much trust in such a vendor, a good number of crises can arise. For example, they may go out of business or increase their rates on you if you only use one vendor. They might run out of the items that you expect them to supply. Where would you be then? This is why there should always be a backup for you. It is smart to write up the contract with your vendors for your own insurance to remain aware of your requirements. This will ensure that everyone involved has agreed to uphold what you demand.

3. Expecting Easy Money.

Dropshipping, as we've already established, offers a degree of ease that can seem to make your work easier. Yet, you can't ignore how critical your product is in marketing and all the competition you're going to face. This involves analysis and the creation of a unique approach that will allow the product more attractive than that of anyone else.

4. Making Order Difficult to Access.

When you assure your consumers a simple and quick procedure, they'll want to see the proofs. Set approximate location-based ship dates and require suppliers to keep you posted on the status of the order so that you can keep the consumer aware. This way, you can track shipments whenever you anticipate them to come longer than expected and easily fix issues.

5. Not Enough Brand Display.

Through dropshipping, it may be hard to guarantee the brand remains to be seen in the customer's overall experience. You may not want people to forget regarding you, so it's important to insert as many locations as possible into your brand. You should have customized packing slips, stickers and custom exterior packaging to hold the name included after delivery. Sending a follow-up thank you message or a survey to remind about of you and prove them you think for their feedback at the same time is also not a bad idea.

6. Return Complications.

If you do not have a system for returns set up, things can get messy very quickly. You and your vendor will have to establish a refund policy to avoid this. Customers are going to wait for their refund expectantly, and being disorganized on that front and will not make them feel good. They may also need guidelines explaining how or where to return the product. Organizing a structure for this will save a good amount of confusion and irritation for both you and the client.

7. Selling Trademarked Products

When most people learn about dropshipping and realize that it is not that complicated to do the process, they picture all the things they might sell and make a quick buck.

Many of these goods are items which have been trademarked by a manufacturer. Selling these goods without the manufacturer's specific consent to be a retail agent will lead you to legal issues. This can not only lead to the end of your online shop, but you can also be held personally responsible.

You should, consequently, look at generic items which you can add to your variety of products for sale. Best still, you should swap in goods with white marks. They are plain goods that are available to those who rebrand them through the manufacturer. You will order and get these items customized to suit the brand and display them.

8. Picking the Wrong Field

Once you have abandoned thoughts of selling any product you come across, by concentrating on one field, you can develop your dropshipping business.

You might, however, select the wrong niche in which to operate. Maybe you should pick a niche that isn't lucrative. This may be that it's out of vogue or it's simply not meant for shopping online.

Therefore, to see what will earn you money, you have to do proper market analysis. "Market research" might sound like a complex process in which only major brands participate.

Simple Google searches will, therefore, show you what individuals are interested in and where they purchase them.

9. Poor Relationship With Suppliers

Your vendors are part of your business; they promise that you have the best goods and that they supply your consumers with them. You can be inclined, though, to consider them as workers and handle them as though they are in the hierarchy on a lower rung.

They're not. They are your friends, without whom it would be effectively dead for your dropshipping business. Therefore, you can establish a better relationship with them.

This will have its benefits. When negotiating costs for commodity stock, a strong partnership will work in your favor.

10. Lowering Price To Extreme Levels

Reducing your prices to knock out your competition is also one of the dropshipping failures to avoid.

This is a logical way for you to rise your dropshipping business, you might think. You could have been no farther from the facts. Very low prices indicate to potential customers that your product may be of poor quality.

11. Poor Website Structure

The progress of your dropshipping company depends on the shopping experience your clients have when they browse your online store.

Thus, you have to make sure everything is convenient for them. However, you could rush through the process of establishing your website due to low barrier for entrance into dropshipping. Many beginners do not have the coding skills required to construct an online store.

In conclusion, the primary interest is the customer's experience. Although inventory management and shipping are not your responsibility, you can also ensure that all is well handled. All of these dropshipping failures can be prevented with adequate preparation and careful management, and the business can better manage.

Chapter 9. Smooth Running tips for Your Dropshipping Business

Well, you've done your research, decided to agree on the right dropship goods and roped in the right possible supplier. All of you are planned to begin dropshipping goods and make the mullah! Setting up the company, though, is typically one thing, but a totally different ball game is to manage it on a day-to-day basis. Even if it's a dropshipping company, there are various facets of running a business that you have to remember as a retailer: marketing, refunds, refunds, repairs, inventory, distribution, customer service, and far more. So dive into all these different aspects of managing a dropshipping business.

So far, when covered a lot of details, it involves everything from the fundamentals of dropshipping to the nuances of finding a niche and managing the business. You should have much of a base by now to begin investigating and establishing your own dropshipping company comfortably.

It's possible to get confused and lose track about what's really necessary, with too much to consider. That's why we've built this list of key elements for success. This are the main "must-do" acts that can make the new company or ruin it. If you can perform these effectively, you would be able to get a bunch of other stuff wrong and yet have a decent probability of success.

1. Add Value

The most important performance element is making a good roadmap on how you will bring value to your clients. In the field of dropshipping, where you can contend with legions of other "me too" stores carrying related items, this is critical for both corporations, but even more so.

With dropshipping, it's reasonable to think you're marketing a product to consumers. Yet good small merchants realize that they are offering insights, ideas and solutions, not just the commodity they deliver. You assume you're an e-commerce seller, but you're in the information industry as well.

If you can't create value by quality data and advice, price is the only thing you're left to contend on. While this has been an effective technique for Walmart, it will not help you grow a successful company for dropshipping.

2. Focus on SEO and marketing

The opportunity to push traffic to the new platform is a near second to providing value as a main key factor. A shortage of traffic to their sites is the #1 concern and annoyance faced by modern e-commerce retailers. So many retailers have been slaving away on the ideal platform for months just to unleash it into a community that has no clue it exists.

For the success of your company, advertising and driving traffic is completely necessary and challenging to outsource well, particularly if you have a limited budget and bootstrap your business. In order to build your own SEO, publicity, outreach and guest posting abilities, you have to consider taking the personal initiative.

Within the first 6 - 12 months, where no one know who you are, this is particularly crucial. You need to devote at least 75 percent of your time on publicity, SEO and traffic development for at least 4 to 6 months after your website launch, which is right, 4 to 6 months. You can start reducing and coast a little on the job you put in until you've built a strong marketing base. But it's difficult, early on, to bring so much emphasis on advertising.

3. Marketing Your Dropshipping Business

Marketing is indeed a subjective field, and that there are a billion strategies which can be used to position your brand successfully whilst driving awareness and sales of your brand. It will even help you root out the remainder of the market if the approach is well planned.

4. Social Media Source

Social networking is one of the most efficient ways to promote, advertise, attract clients and share content, so when social networks are now used for digital marketing, it comes as no surprise. For example, Facebook has more than 1.7 billion active members from diverse walks of life, and it is this diversity that makes it so appealing to online marketers.

One thing to note is that it's important to content. No matter how perfect a platform is or how good the product you are offering is, without high quality content backing it up, it means nothing.

5. Customer Ratings & Reviews

A few bad customer ratings will actually ruin a business in dropshipping business model. Think about it: As you order online from websites like ebay and aliexpress, the quality ranking and what other consumers had to tell about it will be one of the determining purchase variables, too, with decrease delivery. A few positive feedback will also give you an advantage over the competition because that is what will help you convert traffic to your website successfully.

6. Email Marketing

In a digital marketer's pack, this one of the most neglected tools. To keep your clients in the loop for any major changes within company, email marketing may be used: Price increases, promotions, coupons, content related to the commodity, and content unique to the industry are only some of the forms email marketing may be utilized.

7. Growth Hacking

Growth hacking is a cheap but highly productive way to get online creative marketing campaigns. A few definitions of growth hacking involve retargeting old campaigns and featuring in your own niche as a guest writer for a popular website. Any of this commonly involves content marketing.

Chapter 10. How To Maximize Your Chances Of Success?

There are only a couple more tips you should adopt to maximize the chances of long-term growth if you are willing to take the plunge and attempt dropshipping. Second, that doesn't mean you can approach a dropshipping business because it's risk-free simply because there are no setup costs involved with purchasing and managing goods. You're also spending a lot of time choosing the right dropshippers while designing your website, so consider it as an investment and do careful preliminary research.

1. Things To Remember

What do you want to sell? How profitable is the surroundings? How can you gain clients and distinguish yourself? Inside the same room, is there a smaller niche that is less competitive? When they find a particular market and curate their goods like a pro, most individuals who operate a purely dropshipping model have seen the most growth, ensuring that any last item they offer is a successful match for their niche audience with their brand.

After you develop your list of possible dropshippers, carry out test orders and then watch for the items to arrive, thinking like a consumer. How long can any order take? What is the feeling of unboxing like? What is the commodity standard itself? This will help you distinguish between possible dropshippers or confirm that positive consumer service is offered by the one you want.

Note that the goods themselves may not be the differentiator for your business.

After you have chosen your dropshippers and products, note that the products themselves may not be the differentiator for your business. So ask what else you should count on to make the deal. This is another explanation why test orders are a wonderful idea since they encourage you to obtain the item and explain its functionality and advantages as a client might. In a way which really shows it off, you can even take high-quality, professional pictures of the product. Armed with exclusive explanations of the goods and images that are separate from all the other product photos, you would be able to start standing out.

Your bread and butter is definitely going to be a well-executed campaign strategy, so devote time and money on each section of it, from finding your potential audience to interacting with influencers on social media in your niche. Targeted commercials can be a perfect way to kick start your site to bring your name on the mind of your client base.

When it relates to your return policies, delivery contact and customer support, ensure your ducks are in a line. You'll need to do what you could to serve as the buffer between a dropshipper and your client if something goes wrong somewhere in the process. Understand the typical cost of return for each item so that you will notice whether it is large enough to denote a quality issue. If you suspect a consistency problem, talk to your dropshipper or try a different supplier to your issues.

Eventually, note that dropshipping is not a model of "all or nothing." Many of the more profitable corporations follow a hybrid model, making or shipping in-house some goods and employing dropshippers to fill the gaps. The dropshippers are not the key profit-drivers for these firms but are instead a simple, inexpensive way to provide clients with the "extras" they can enjoy. Before you put it in-house, you can even use dropshipped products for upsells, impulse sales, or to try a new model.

As long as you consider the above tips to ensuring that the one you chose is suitable for your business needs, there is definitely a lot to learn from the streamlining and flexibility of using a dropshipper. You will make your dropshipping store run for you in no time with a little of research, negotiation, and setup!

Conclusion

So that concludes our definitive dropshipping guide. You now learn how to set up to kick start your new dropshipping business if you've made it here. Starting up your own business often involves a certain degree of dedication, effort, and ambition to make things work, much as in every other undertaking in life. It's not only about building the business but also about pushing through and knowing how to manage it on a daily basis.

The greatest feature of dropshipping is that you will practice in real-time by checking your goods and concepts, and all you have to do is drop it from your shop if anything doesn't work. This business concept is indeed a perfect opportunity for conventional business models to try out product concepts. Dropshipping creates a secure place to innovate to see what happens without incurring any substantial damages that will surely give business owners the courage to state that they have a working idea of how the market works. The dropshipping business model is an interesting business model to move into with little initial expense and relatively little risk.

A perfect choice to drop shipping if you are only starting to sell online and would like to test the waters first. It's a great way to start your business, even if the margins are low.

As dropshipping can still get started with little investment, before they build their market image, businessmen can start with that too. Ecommerce sites such as Ebay, Shopify, Alibaba and social networking, such as Instagram, Twitter, Reddit, provide vast expertise in user base and content marketing. It also helps newbies to

84

know about establishing an online store, optimizing conversions, generating traffic and other basics of e-commerce.

That's what you need to learn about beginning a dropshipping. Just note, it's not the hard part to launch your dropshipping store, the real challenge is when you get trapped, and your stuff is not being sold. Do not panic, and keep checking as it happens. You're going to get a product soon that sells well.

Youtube, Tik-Tok and Instagram Made Easy

A Collection of Filters, Entertaining Topics and Viral Trends to Gain 10k Followers and Generate Passive Income

By

Nespy Online Marketing

Table of contents

Introduction

Don't think you can compete against millions of creators and influencers? Well, let's set one thing straight, not only can you do it but also how you can do it. Working smarter, not necessarily harder, makes all the difference.

This book is for those who wish to make a name of themselves by leaving behind a reputation, legacy on social media platforms. Or maybe, all you want is to be able to do what you love for a living and offer that to the world. Either way, you're in the right place.

If you haven't been able to make much of a passive income from these social platforms for a while now, you should know it's probably not you; it's the platform. This book aims to provide an insight into these social platforms by teaching you how to increase your audience by changing some basic habits and teach you a few new tips, tricks, and tactics you can use by first understanding their working. 10,000 is perhaps the right number of followers to be considered literally as an influencer/brand, get paying offers, and raise your account's value.

It may be sluggish as you try to win the starting few followers, but it does get a little easier after that. Understanding the algorithm plays a crucial role in enlarging your audience. YouTube, Tik Tok, and Instagram use algorithms to recommend various creators. Once you understand how their algorithms work, you can easily reach a larger variety of users. By gaining an active audience of about 10K, YouTube, Tik Tok, and Instagram may consider paying attention to your content, and you could even gain more than 10,000 depending on your consistency.

Now, you are probably thinking "easier said than done", right? Well, don't worry, this book is solely there to make these things easier. To provide a how-to gain 10K followers quickly, An easy-to-use reference to aid your growth on social media platforms (i.e., YouTube, Tik Tok, and Instagram.)

Try not to read this book as a novel; rather, truly study it and apply it in your daily practices to notice change and improvement in your channel/account/profile growth.

First, this book will teach you why earning a passive income through YouTube, Tik Tok, and Instagram is the way to go, especially in this day and age, next, how each platform has its own way of working and different method to win over the platform to your side. And then, if you're having a tough time generating content for these platforms, the last part will teach you how you can remove your creativity block and let your muse come to you. Last but not least, Afterthoughts will give you that push you need to get cracking, radiating motivation and energy to really get you started.

CHAPTER I: Why it's One of the Best Ways to Earn

In current times, the Internet is available in almost every part of the world. People interact, learn, and enjoy through platforms. More specifically, YouTube, Tik Tok, and Instagram. Since 2020, most people have spent their time at home, and so usage of these social media platforms has grown excessively. People discovered hidden talents, curiosity, and inspiration so much more than before.

Even if people hadn't spent half their time on their phones or other electronic devices, there are so many advantages of working on YouTube, Tik Tok, and Instagram for a passive income.

1.1: Freedom of Speech

YouTube, Tik Tok, and Instagram are the kind of social media platforms that allow an individual to really do anything and everything they want, needless to say, as long as they follow community guidelines.

"I do not agree with what you have to say, but I'll defend to the death your right to say it." ~ Voltaire

From a thriller, a short film to kids toy reviews, from gameplays to reactions, whatever. These are platforms where even the smallest of people have a voice, and they can make it known. Your creativity can literally pay the bills and put food on the table. And there can always be an endless supply of creativity, that is if you know where to look.

What could you possibly want more than being able to do what you love for a living? It's the ideal dream. And there are so many advantages of being able to do what you enjoy for a living.

High Efficiency

You become more useful and productive with your work as you can be excited for the next day. Your work won't even feel like a job, and so you would find yourself more relaxed as it wouldn't feel like a burden, finding other things to do in your spare time would be exciting too.

Inspiration

When you're having a tough time, doing what you love can spark inspiration and motivation in you. Once you feel inspired, your ideas run like a high-quality car engine, and it can sometimes even get difficult to do all these amazing things you have in mind.

New Perspectives

When you are following a boring schedule every single day and spend most of your time thinking about what you would do once the weekends here, you should realize you're doing it wrong. When working on a social media platform, you don't have a boss; in fact, you are your own boss, much like running a business. You set timings that are best suited for your work, and as being a public figure is constantly exciting, you won't find yourself in the same routine each day. Sure, you would probably have some ups and downs, but at the end of the day, you work for your own satisfaction and so view life from a different point of view than those who work solely because they feel they have no choice.

Better Wellbeing

Working on your chosen niche on these social platforms sounds fun and enjoyable, and it is. What you probably didn't know that being happy is great for your health. In fact, it's a lot cheaper than being miserable and stressed for every day of your life. It even relieves all that stress, mental and physical tension.

1.2: Fame

An Audience

Working on being a public figure or influencer gives you an audience that cares for you; they show an interest in your content. It could make you a role model for them, or they see your content to put a smile on their faces, it could help them in some basic struggles they didn't know they had until they saw your work.

Your followers/subscribers may value your opinions on certain topics and appreciates you and your content in the respective niche. And being validated for your effort would make anyone happy.

They even help you grow by giving honest feedback and so you can easily tell what it is they like about your content.

Opportunities

Fame grants you several chances to work with well-known brands or companies. Whether that be in sponsored advertisements or partnerships for products (i.e., perfume, apparel, electronic gadgets, games, etc.)

For example, maybe you're a sports-focused content creator, you could get offers from sportswear companies to model with their products!

Not only brands but also popular public figures would notice you, and you'd be given numerous opportunities to work with them, especially if you're in the same niche as them. When an already successful creator acknowledges and validates your content, they bring in their fans to your work, ultimately broadening your audience.

For instance, YouTuber Lilly Singh, also known as superwoman, grew so big on YouTube that she now hosts a late-night show called "A Little Late with Lilly Singh" on NBC. She not only released a film that entailed her world tour but also a book named "How to Be a Bawse: A Guide to Conquering Life," which made it to New York Times best-seller list. She also won a substantial number of rewards on multiple award shows over the years and made her own music videos, and so much more. Her Niche? Entertainment. And it's an understatement to say she entertained.

@lilly with @malala Via Instagram

Of course, it didn't come easy to her, but with time, her channel grew and not only on YouTube but also across other platforms like Instagram.

Like her, once you obtain that loyal audience, you could try new things whenever you want, but not too much, or you may drive your audience away. You'd be able to work on creative projects. (i.e., Liza Koshy acted in a tv show and other showbiz related content, PewDiePe who made not one but two games with another company as well as a YouTube original show called "Scare PewDiePie", Joey Graceffa who made his own YouTube original show called "Escape the Night".)

1.3: Money

The obvious reason for earning through YouTube, Tik Tok, and Instagram? The Money. Succeeding on any social platform often promises good fortune. Influencers often buy new cars, houses, editors to help them with their work, maybe even a new oven!

You'd finally be able to finish that bucket list. Get something for the people you care about! And most importantly, once you get that money you've been waiting for, be grateful and don't take it for granted.

YouTubers like Lilly Singh made use of their money by making her profile a little more professional by hiring a team and basically becoming a CEO of her team. A lot of influencers do live charity streams, raise money, or donate for the poor and needy in several ways as well. Well, that's not all she did with her money she spent it for fun too as I'm sure you can as well do whatever you want with it.

Merchandising

You would be able to sell your own products, which would be your signature merch (people would recognize it as yours). Often influencers get sweatshirts, T-shirts, caps, posters, phone covers, etc. This increases your profits as well as advertising yourself. You get something to represent yourself with and receive more recognition.

CHAPTER II: YouTube

2.1: How it Works

To know how to easily get 10,000 subscribers on YouTube, you first need to be able to understand the YouTube software's working and how you can use it to your advantage.

Video

YouTube is a free space where creators can store videos, pictures, and posts. But their main focus is the videos that various people of all types upload. Google owns it, and its search engine is the second largest around the globe. YouTube videos can be embedded into other websites as well.

Moreover, YouTube recommends videos that are viewed by a similar audience to the one a user is currently watching.

Being successful through YouTube won't happen in a week. You have to be prepared to go through the rough patches as well as the smooth ones.

Analytics

There is a reporting, and self-service analytics tool on YouTube which provides intel regarding every video you upload so YouTube can help you easily keep track of how many views each video receives, what type of people are watching your content (age group, where they are from, and such).

It can provide data about:

1. The age groups and genders it is commonly seen by.

2. The statistics: comments, ratings, and views.

3. The countries your content is mostly seen in.

4. The first time your video was recommended to a user, either when they are watching something similar or when your video was recommended when they search a keyword.

5. In the first instance, your video was embedded in a website by a third party.

Advertising

YouTube embeds features that allow various businesses to promote their content to users who may have an interest in it, aiming at clients by subject and demographics.

The advertisers pay you each time someone in your audience views their Ad. They can decide the areas in which the Ad will show, the amount of payment, and the format.

Channels

Create your own niche, don't constantly jump from one genre to another, or your audience will never remain consistent.

2.2: The Content

Watch Time

Videos that consist of a higher watch time get recommended frequently on the main YouTube homepage. So how do you increase it? Pattern Interrupts.

These result in making your videos more vibrant, which prolongs the viewers' attention span.

A pattern interrupt can be jump cuts, graphics, different camera angles, and cheesy humor. It can put a smile on the watcher's face or catch them off guard, which keeps them watching.

Trends

Keeping up with the current times is vital for small channels to grow. Trends are one of the catalysts of increasing your audience.

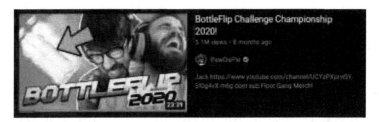

PewDiePie Via YouTube

As of February 2021, most YouTubers stream live, do how-to tutorials, DIY's, etc.

Things like the chubby bunny challenge, Reddit reactions (cross-platform), spicy foods challenge, etc., gives more room for the creator and audience to get to know one another. The goal is to make them feel like your friend, so they feel comfortable enough to come back.

Create longer videos.

Making long videos (10+ minutes) actually gives your video a higher rank in YouTube's search results in most cases. Of course, if you make the video longer with not much to add, then it will still be lowly ranked as users will prefer not to waste their time.

And definitely avoid making videos longer than an hour because it's likely the viewers' attention gets diverted.

Like, Share, and Subscribe

At any point of the video, remind your viewers to subscribe, but make sure you don't keep mentioning that along with 'Like, Share, and hit the notification bell' as this tends to irritate the viewers due to the fact that they just want to watch the video. Keep the message short and maybe even humorous to attract the viewers.

Link more videos at the end.

If the users watch more of *your* content, they will probably subscribe. So, promoting your videos will definitely increase the chances of them watching it as it would be convenient for them to just click on that instead of going to your channel and surfing through there.

Quality over Quantity

Viewers can never be fooled by the number of videos you upload every week, they value the effort and time put into each piece of content, and they are well aware that you are as human as they are.

Do try maintaining a schedule just to let your viewers know when they can expect a video, but don't force it, or it will not be valued.

Thumbnail and Video Title

Your thumbnails should be eye-catching and interesting, as it is the first thing they see when they are introduced to your channel. It's your first impression. Make sure it's a high-quality image.

If it's a professional website, a simple and sleek thumbnail will do. If it's a vlog or an entertainment purpose video, an exciting title with an image of the most important part of the video in place of the thumbnail would fit nicely.

For example, if you want to give your review on a certain product, give a strong statement as a title that would be intriguing for people to watch (i.e., 'Why I think the new Tesla cars are amazing', 'Why Harry Potter actually makes no sense', 'Public Speaker Reacts to PewDiePie')

More Content

At the end of your videos, hint at what you'll be doing next so your viewers can come back for more.

Keep track of your subscriber magnet. In analytics, creators can see what type of videos made by you have the most views. So, start by focusing on those. Obviously, don't make a hundred parts on the same topic, but keeping track of your subscriber magnet can help a lot.

2.3: Channel Profile

Keep an attractive and creative Channel with intriguing art styles, so it shows the work put in your banner. It welcomes the viewers. Here are some examples:

Jaclyn Lovey Via YouTube: here, Jaclyn made a minimalistic banner with her video update schedule and her genre of videos mentioned, so newcomers do not have to search for it; convenience.

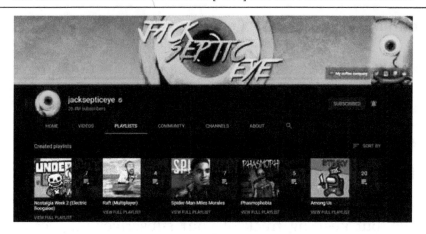

jacksepticeye Via YouTube: Jack, a successful YouTuber with over 20 Million views, categorized all his videos in playlists so users can access any genre of his videos anytime. Also, notice a signature logo, and he mentioned all his handles, brand links too.

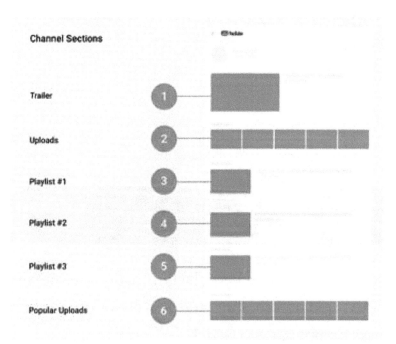

Make an exciting and persuading channel trailer. Preferably short and catchy, show the best you can here because these viewers came specifically to your channel, and you want to keep them there.

Organize the Channel page in a way that's convenient to the viewers.

Check out this basic layout:

Mention other platforms you use so they keep up with you if they don't rely on YouTube.

In 'About', make sure you provide at least 300 words about yourself, what kind of content you put out into the world, and why you think they'd be interested. If you have an upload schedule (please do), then mention that as well. Persuade the viewers to subscribe by the end of it. Keeping a polite tone in your descriptions, whether it be a channel description or video description, gives the viewer a positive and kind tone. They wouldn't particularly enjoy watching someone who talks in a manner of giving orders rather than guiding or entertaining (depending on your content subject).

Make sure you use well-known keywords that describe your content. (i.e., Crash courses, funny, motivational, etc.) so the YouTube algorithm can detect these things. Here's an easy comparison:

A:

Via YouTube

B: Via YouTube

Which is a better Description of the YouTuber? I hope you say B, because it is, in fact, B.

Categorize your videos into playlists. For example, if you are running a gaming channel, make sure long gameplays are divided into separate videos but put together in one playlist after you upload them. Not many people watch 4-hour gameplays all at once, especially when you are starting as a small channel. But suppose you divide your gameplays into videos and edit them to cut out the boring bits. In that case, they may enjoy watching multiple short videos, which would be around 15-20 minutes each- depending on your preferences.

2.4: Interactivity

Replying to comments is the best and simplest way to gain more subscribers. The more you interact with your viewers and give importance to their feedback, the longer they stay.

"When creators take the time to interact with their local community, it can encourage audience participation and ultimately result in a larger fanbase." ~ YouTube.

Creator Hearts- you can heart your favorite comments to recognize comments from your public. By doing this, the viewer gets a notification, and this keeps interactivity high by leading them back to your channel. These notifications receive 300% additional clicks than normal.

Once you get a handful of people that are consistent in watching your content, you can even ask for their opinion on anything related to the video or even an idea for the next video. To engage your community is perhaps the most important thing, especially when you are a growing channel. Doing Q&A videos every once in a while acknowledges the audience and engages them more.

Recently, YouTube updated, and now Creators can interact with their audience with polls and posts as well as comments. Using these frequently to keep your audience there is vital.

Shine Theory

Needless to say, they'd be more excited by a famous YouTuber replying to their comments, but you could be famous soon enough too! So, building a community that promotes each other does help. This concept comes from the Shine Theory.

Shine Theory is a long-term investment, where two individuals, creators, or consumers, help each other by means of advertising or engagement depending on the platform it is being used.

CHAPTER III: *Tik Tok*

3.1: Down the Rabbit Hole

Over 2 billion people have downloaded Tik Tok all around the globe. Especially during the global pandemic, literally, everyone seems to have this app on their phone- and even if they don't have the app, it is taking over the apps they *do* have.

Tik Tok is super addicting, and the main reason for this is that each video is no longer than one minute, which gives viewers quick entertainment / tips / motivation.

Tik Tok famous is a word the vast majority seems to be throwing around as if it is a solid career, but the problem is, they all act as though it's a comfortable ride without even putting their back into it! Though it's a little more complicated than that, and you'd know that. But don't worry, here's a step-by-step guide to how you can be Tik Tok famous in no time.

This is the kind of platform that anyone can get into, from a 7-year-old to a 70-year-old *anyone.* Most people follow overnight after one of your Tik Tok's go mega-viral. Without further ado, let's start with all the things you need to remember to get 10 000 followers on Tik Tok.

3.2: The Algorithm

The Tik Tok algorithm was updated recently at the start of 2021, due to which a number of views on Tik Toks have started to go down. They did this because Tik Tok realized Tik Toks could go viral for almost anyone and a lot of creators' content was against community guidelines, so the early adopter advantage is lost. A way to tackle this is- keep pumping out more content. These algorithms will keep updating throughout the years, but the best you can do is give the viewers a reason to watch.

3.3: Your Profile

Username

Choose a simple yet unique username. One that is familiar to your niche would be most preferred as it would make users find you conveniently. (i.e., if your Tik Toks are travel-focused, you can call yourself JourneysInLife)

Bio

Think of an intriguing Profile Bio. Something welcoming, relatable, original, fun, and interesting your followers would enjoy. And definitely mention your niche to clarify your target audience. Often really good bios consist of a call to action (i.e., follow for a cookie).

Upload a Photo (high-quality image not to look cheap). Link your other social media handles like Instagram, YouTube, etc.

3.4: The Content

Target Audience

Before blindly making videos, you need to consider what kind of audience you're aiming for. Firstly, they use Tik Tok. If you think editing videos the same way you'd edit a YouTube or IGTV video will work, you're wrong. Every platform is unique in its own significant way, so you need to pay attention to how Tik Tok is entertaining and focuses on that.

Is it family-friendly content for youngsters? Short tutorials for artists? Perhaps it's professional cooking for beginners. You need to think about your audience's geolocation, age group, gender, so on and so forth.

This is an approximate age breakdown:

- Age 55+: 5%

- Age 44-53: 2%

- Age 34-43: 7%

- Age 24-33: 15%

- Age 17-23: 41%

- Age 13-16: 26%

What's your Niche?

Delivering high-quality videos (in both quality of the video and content) is the most basic important thing. Don't steal content from other underrated creators, or it will have dire consequences like getting banned.

Make it unique, edit your videos with your ability if you can because people get tired of seeing the same editing design used by the Tik Tok app. There are various editing apps
like ViaMaker, Zoomerang, Quik, InShot, Funimate, etc.

Quality

You need a really powerful hook in the first 3 seconds the keep the viewers wanting to watch more. Your job is to do everything and anything to keep the viewers from clicking away then make them interested enough to follow!

To do this, you need a significant number of pattern interrupts-graphics, different camera angles, etc. It could be as easy as starting with a greeting or as concrete as taking the time to explore or finishing your wish list. A trend disrupts you to exciting new locations, both visually and psychologically. It jolts you away from your comfortable perceptions and rituals and then into broad freedom of possibilities.

Better quality videos are pleasing to the eye, and they will likely continue watching until it ends. Sometimes Tik Tok degrades your videos' quality, and the reason this happens is that the data saved on your app has been turned on often than naught. This feature is on means the Tik Tok application downloads your mobile data while you watch videos. This decreases the resolution of your clips too. So, to tackle this, you can turn off the data saver feature.

Collabs

Collaborating with some people you have good chemistry with really improves shares as it would be increasing both your and the other Tik Tokers views/follows another branch of Shine Theory.

Not just that, but Tik Tok allows you to reply to other influencers Tik Tok with your own, right? Use that! Make your reply unique and interesting to get them and other viewers to notice.

When it comes to collaborations with companies, sponsorships sound nice but try not to overdo it. While looking for new celebrities to partner with, be sure to review how many supported videos are posted. When a majority of their latest material is paying for updates, their commitment rate will not last. Alternatively, search for influencers with a decent amount of organic, non-sponsored material. As they probably have fans interested and involved.

Going Viral

When you post a video on Tik Tok, your creativity has the potential to ignite a chain reaction.

To get a decent amount of exposure, engage in trends, challenges, and duets. Put your own twists on patterns that captivate individuals. Paying attention to and bookmarking popular clips can prove useful to use it for inspiration. In Tik Tok, there are so many viral challenges. Engaging in various challenges will increase your visibility to the network and encourage you to get far more follows.

On the majority of your Tik Toks, for now, at least, use recommended and trending songs. Positive content almost always has more views, something quirky and enjoyable with a warm tone. Using a trending song is the next move (except when your music is original or a video idea in particular to a kind of sound.)

This is the reason why using trending songs is clever: basically, Tik Tok is a little wired in regard to trending songs to promote videos. It wasn't a random occurrence that Tik Tok also works with record companies; they work together to promote the artist's music in the app to improve the sales of the album and raise the likelihood that the song can hit the top rankings. Tik Tok practically dominates the music world. A mere peek at the week's Top 100 tunes. Most of those best hits on Tik Tok are those that are mega-famous. How do you know what tunes everyone's listening to? Simply choose one of the suggested tracks the platform recommends when you make your film.

Get on top of all those trends, except with a surprise. Do the idea of popular dances or rising clips, but add a twist on it and make it something of your own. You need to balance trending videos with fresh material when you're a small producer. A Tik Tok clip received millions of views, and that account got about 10,000 Tik Tok followers; it just happened overnight.

However, once you receive those views, you shouldn't anticipate the next day to be filled with that much fame, because you will probably be disappointed. Once you get over a million views, then you need to keep up the work or probably work even harder than before to keep everyone there.

Make sure you don't take part in really cringe trends, though!

Using Hashtags

Utilize hashtags as much as you can, especially hashtags that are trending. This actually matters because the Tik Tok algorithm detects these hashtags and recommends your content accordingly.

The cleverer and simpler your hashtags are, the higher your videos get ranked on Tik Tok, which in result increases your views and likes. Along with being in contact with record labels, Tik Tok often works with companies/brands, and their drives are almost always attached with a hashtag. This encourages your videos on people's For You Page during the duration of the campaigns.

1-2 hashtags are preferred. Go to the Discover tab and take 1-2 trending and 1-2 broad hashtags or tags related to your related to you exclusively and trendy.

Most Popular: #tiktokers #lfl #bhfyp #follow #explorepage #followforfollowback #explore #meme #tiktokdance #viral #memes #tiktokindia #photography #tiktokindonesia #k #cute #art #youtube #instagood #fashion #likes #bhfyp #likeforlikes #trending #music #funny #tiktok #instagram #love #like

Timing Matters!

What time you decide to post your content actually matters. When most people are online is when you'd want to put out videos and this depends on your geolocation heavily. If you're careful, you can get twice the followers you'd normally get.

Posting late at night (not too late), afternoon, and early morning tend to be the best times as most people would be looking through their phones then.

But that's just an average. To be more specific, go into your account analytics and content section, look at the past 7 days and what times your content was viewed most often, then make your posting times according to when your most interactive followers were active to make it as convenient for them as possible. Also, take into consideration the timings more well-known Tik Tokers in your niche are posting.

Repost and Share.

Sometimes, your video doesn't do as well the first time but reposting it several times a day and week can drastically change that because sometimes your followers just miss it. Saying things like 'Posting again till it goes viral' or 'Reposting since it didn't do too well last time' can really make a difference.

Sharing your videos on every other social media platform (i.e., Instagram, Twitter, Facebook, etc.)

Engagement

You need to turn your viewers, commenters, and likers into followers, especially at such an early stage. Basically, your early squad needs the spa treatment. To do this, perhaps the most important thing is engaging with your community. Interacting with them as much and as often as you can is vital to Tik Tok's growth.

Reply to each and every comment. People love viewing comments seeing their opinion was acknowledged would be a satisfying feeling for everyone. Credits: wired

Follow everyone, and I mean everyone that has interacted with your account in any way.

Go Live every single day, and it really boosts your page. Even if you're super busy, go live and work!

If you receive hate comments, reply back with a bit of humor! However, if it's constructive criticism, show interest, and try actually considering their opinion, this can really help your account develop.

Ask questions in your videos, so they feel the need to reply in the comments. This is a little trick most creators use.

Staying Consistent

Posting regularly is important. Post multiple times a day (considering the timings) and try avoiding uploading content right after each other, or it will not be pushed to the For You page.

Stockpile videos: If you have a day off, film as much content as you can so you can still upload videos if you're too busy another day. Posting 3-6 times a day is an ideal amount.

Duration

The duration of each video is preferred to be 11-17 sec long. The ideal time for something to be pushed out into the algorithm. And you'd get a good amount of watch time. Keep it shorter than you think it needs to be.

Tik Tok revolves around fun and concise videos, so if yours is too long than they would like, Tik Tok may decrease your rank on the For You page.

Ask them to follow, like, and comment.

The easiest method to improve the number of followers you have is by asking the viewers to 'double tap!' or 'let me know what you think in the comment section'; these things remind viewers to give you some sort of feedback on the content you create.

Asking for engagement in every video for a *very* brief period of time in the video and saying it in the description is important. Make sure it isn't mentioned for longer than 2-3 seconds, or the viewer will get bored and click away.

Keep all your content accessible.

Never delete any of your Tik Tok videos because it's likely your posts won't do well right away; you need to give it time. Your previous posts can go viral any time, so never keep them private or delete them.

There have been many times a Tik Toker posts a video, and it gets hardly 500 views in the first night, but about a few weeks later, it starts to become trending again, and you get a thousand more views.

Judge Yourself

Not to the point, you put yourself down, of course, but realistically judging yourself to keep track of your work is important.

How will this video contribute to your growth?

Is it interesting for people in my own niche?

Why would it be interesting?

What themes can I use to make this better?

If the most popular Tik Toker in my niche saw this, would they be impressed?

Take these things into consideration when you're done with certain Tik Toks.

Follow Guidelines

Especially with the recent 2021 update, you don't want to get on Tik Tok's bad side. Make sure you aren't copying someone else's work on your own profile, as that would really degrade your account.

Funded partnerships may not be as clear to Tik Tok as they are to other social networking sites, but that wouldn't imply that the very same FTC laws do not apply. Tik Tok celebrities are expected to report advertising with a transparent and obvious message that the material is funded or promoted.

Do not, under any circumstance, attempt to get free followers. This will never help you really grow. And it can have really adverse consequences later on if you are serious about Tik Tok as this is seen as a way to steal from Tik Tok. Trying to buy free followers will never get you the triumph you thrive for.

Stitch- The Tik Tok Feature

This adds yet another way for the user to interact with material that is created and posted every day by the creative Tik Tok users. Stitch is a feature the company called which enables a user to put in snippets of another Tik Tok video in yours.

How can you use it?

1. Search for the video you want to stitch and then click on 'Send to'.

2. Click on 'Stitch'

3. You can pull only 5 seconds out of the video, so choose wisely.

4. Make the rest of the video you want to put in with the stitched snippet.

5. Stitch them all together!

In the settings menu, you may select if you want to allow others to stitch your material. This is accessible on the Security and Confidentiality tab underneath "Settings and Privacy." You could allow or remove Stitch for any of your clips. Conversely, this feature can be customized for every clip you post.

Stay Stress-free

Don't try to push out more content forcefully, if your audience sees that you are, they would easily be able to get that your content came from a negative mindset. Keep it fun, enjoy making the clips, actually show your positivity.

Having a healthy mindset further nurtures your creativity and gets your ideas flowing, and you need as much of that as possible. Being authentic with your followers is key.

A few different tactics that have proved effective, such as constructive self-discuss and positive envisioning, can achieve encouraging thought.

Here are a few tactics that would prove beneficial for you to prepare your brain in thinking positively to get you started with generating content.

Concentrate on the good stuff. A part of our life is inconvenient situations and obstacles. Look at the constructive stuff once you're faced with one, regardless of how minor or relatively meaningless they are. You may still discover the ultimate positive aspect of any inconvenience if you search for it, even if it's not readily apparent.

Train with appreciation. Studying kindness has been shown to alleviate depression, boost self-esteem and promote endurance in some very trying situations. Image friends, experiences, or stuff that give you any type of warmth or delight, and struggle to convey your thanks at least once every day. This could be a thank you to a co-worker for assisting with a job, to a significant one for cleaning dishes, or to your cat for the affection they have provided.

Keep a diary of thanks. Research studies have reported that putting down stuff you're thankful for will boost your motivation and your state of wellness. You could do that by writing in a thankful diary daily or by setting down a range of items that you're happy for the days when you're going through a rough time. Using this to generate ideas even if it's really far-fetched should prove useful.

Find your motivation, whether that be intrinsic or extrinsic. You get to create the kind of content you like on Tik Tok, any kind! Use that as your passion and drive to work harder and do better.

Let's take a look at a few Tik Tokers

Daniel here has already made 10 parts of the same category and he still has millions of views. Why? Because he doesn't do the *same thing each* time of course, he changes it up, builds better for the next parts. His idea is original, unique, and entertaining!

But be careful not to overdo it, you can't go making 50 parts of the same theme as that would really just stretch it out too much and no one enjoys a guest who overstays their welcome.

daniel.labelle ✓ Daniel LaBelle

If people lagged. Part 10

♫ original sound - Daniel LaBelle

♥

2.9M

💬

16.3K

➤

50.8K

daniel.labelle Via TikTok

Zach shows a clip of the most absurd idea there is: fishing in your house, using these surprises and then a pattern interrupt which involves him falling into the water really is an odd sight to see though very entertaining and unique.

Because of this, a large number of people shared his video and commented in it to share their thoughts.

zachking Via TikTok

CHAPTER IV: *Instagram*

4.1: About You

Instagram is used by everyone in almost every part of the world. It's so popular because Instagram uses imagery rather than text, and people are extra quick to respond to that. It's easier to understand and process visual data rather than heaps of words. And so, visual marketing is blowing up.

The main focus on Instagram is are images. Captions are put out of the way and under the image for that exact reason.

Portrait photography is perhaps the most popular amongst the flock of imageries on Instagram. And most of these images are almost always edited by third-party applications (i.e., Snapseed, VSCO, Adobe Photoshop Express, Polarr).

Not just images, but also Boomerangs, IGTV videos, filters (of which most are created by users), stories, etc. These things push engagement to the front lines.

Naturally, every time Instagram's algorithm changes, it impacts every person who accesses it. You need to make sure you aren't going against the current of those waves. Because the fact is that their algorithm is constantly judging posts all over the globe and deciding which users can see each moment they open the app.

Instagram's algorithm works on machine learning, which makes the way your posts are ranked constantly changing. This book has the most recent details about how to deal with the algorithm to push you further in the marketing campaign and to keep developing engagement with your followers.

Ever since Instagram halted the inverted response in 2016, each specific feed on the site has been arranged as per the algorithm's guidelines.

As per the official @creators handle of Instagram, this concluded in a pleasant result for everybody. Basically, saying they won't be changing it back.

4.2: Ranking Factors

Genre/Niche

Design your account, configure it in a way people can know precisely what they can expect from you. After which, you post intriguing content that your audience will enjoy instantly. If people have liked those kinds of posts before, the system is much more likely to display them.

For example, Let's say Steven came in contact with a verified account. He will probably see more posts from that account, especially if he saw more content from there.

Simply put, users who communicate with content similar to yours are probably going to come across your account as well.

Timing

Recent posts are always going to be recommended more than others. So, just like Tik Tok, posting in timing when your followers are normally active is vital.

People who spend over an hour scrolling on Instagram are obviously going to see numerous kinds of posts from top to bottom compared to someone who spends hardly a few minutes will only see only the top-ranked ones.

Instagram portrays the best at the top of users' feed every time the user activates the application. So, someone who follows hundreds of thousands of accounts will most likely miss a fair number of posts from people they are even really close to.

Engaging Your Audience

Just like every other social media platform, Instagram wishes for users to stay on the app as much and as long as possible as long as they are interested. As an end result, the software cranks up profiles in which the followers are already conversing. This guarantees that the stress on community participation is essential for advertisers and developers.

Credits: mavsocial.com

Sliding in DMs, tagging one another in blogs, and consistently posting comments all are acts that imply a strong bond among users as well as likes, shares, and views.

4.3: What You Need to Do

Pay Attention.

Seeing your Instagram stats is, perhaps shockingly, a few of the easiest ways to get insight into not only how your viewers think but also how the application looks at you.

Could you send everyone much of the same, or twists on the subject? Will they want better photos or videos? Just how many views come from hashtags? What kind of content is going to wow the audience?

Insights tell you did well, so it's up to you to work out where to run from that performance.

Keep It Coming

Some type of involvement, and figuring out where the intended crowd is. To have a grip on the Instagram algorithm, you have to create bonds with your followers first. And because the volume is simple to compute and accomplish than performance, the first item on the agenda is to create a social media posting schedule to stay on track.

What is consistency? Mean for Instagram? This is exclusive to your niche. As you just started, start with the way you want to progress. Think about what's affordable for the team to create.

If you draw viewers with a spark, three stories, two posts, and one IGTV video per day produced a certain amount of perception. Volume and layout selections would depend on the resources you currently have. And what's most critical, however, is to concentrate on publishing posts that you feel proud of regularly.

Reposting is Key.

Even after you have a nice schedule, you're following and knowing what your followers expect, pushing content out into the world isn't simple like butter on jam. Recycle, change-up your best work. Now, not only do you know Instagram wants it, but it also saves a lot of time.

You could transform the videos to gifs, similar pictures to a slideshow, and use pictures used in another photo shoot for multiple reasons, throwbacks, and repost on stories.

Just use the same thing but be extra creative with it.

Collaborating with Other Influencers & Brands

Keep an eye on what other public figures in your niche are up to, and if possible, try to do a collab with them.

Perhaps the easiest way to naturally broaden your scope to fresh eyes is to seek a suitable friend with a complimentary following while still attracting the viewers' interest with appropriate different perspectives. The outcome may very well provide an added strength from Instagram if the partnership is as enjoyable for your community as it would be for you.

Though you need to make sure that the person you choose to partner with is suitable and legitimate, as other influencers will judge you based on who you collab with, it is probably best if you do a detailed background check before setting a collab date with them.

As that influencer will be bringing in their audience, you need to see what kind of followers they have and their analytics. Making sure you don't bring in the wrong crowd who would go away as soon as they came. You could check this by looking at their engagement on posts. If the person you are intending to collab with is genuine and interactive with his/her audience, you should probably go for it.

As searching through every single person, you could collab with would take a significant amount of time, you could use means like Ninjaoutreach, Meltwater, GroupHigh, Newswire, Cision Communications Cloud, etc. This software allows you to make your listing in its database, making things a lot more convenient for you as time is, in fact, of the essence.

The kinds of sponsorships you could get fall into three basic categories: large accounts (120K followers) get at least $400 per sponsored post, middle-class (3K-100K followers) get at least $150, and small accounts (less than 3K) get around $100 or less.

After making a list of the sponsorships you'd like to go for, you need to send each one your pitch. But not in the first text, of course, that would be not polite. Tell them why you're interested in the subject they put out and communicate with them. Once you know what they want exactly, you could develop an amazing pitch.

Next, you need to plan your influencer publicizing campaign. Make sure you keep interacting with the influencers so you can get an insight into what they think. Consider other people's opinions to make a master plan using the influencers and your creativity.

As soon as you have initiated your campaign, please keep track of how it's doing and keep adjusting it accordingly.

An example:

@omayazein partnered up with a brand called Modanisa and gave her audience a discount code, which in turn gets a lot of shares, and she has about 1 Million followers!

@omayazein Via Instagram

Reward Them

As discussed before, Instagram values engagement A LOT, so give your audience what they want! When your audience shares your posts on story or DM, comments and likes push your posts to the top instantly.

The goal should be to create a kind of commitment and passion that motivates individuals to advocate and empower themselves. The service could do the job for you if you already have an outstanding Business-to-consumer service. Anything other than that, you would need to find means of subtly encouraging individuals.

Please stop posting everything sent to you from your community. Compile the latest and integrate material into the digital plan of your content whenever appropriate. And bear in mind that merely reposting the stories of other users has also been specifically noted as something that would not include your stories on the Explore List, so make sure you remain imaginative and on topic.

Like your followers' and viewers' comments, reply to each one, even the haters. Try getting into a conversation with them. Interact with them through stories, polls, use trending filters.

Ask questions on your stories and share them, be humorous, genuine, everything and anything interesting. It could be 'what's your opinion on....' Or 'what's your most embarrassing story!', etc.

If they reply to your stories, make sure you reply!! And not after days at a time, but as soon as you can. Enjoy your time with them. Really try and understand what they wish to see from you. Unless they're just there to hate on you, then you should probably ignore it or if you could do something creative with it (while following community guidelines), go for it.

Follow influencers that are familiar with your niche. This can link other people that are interested in your type of content to you. Not just follow, but also like and comment on their posts, share it!

(Another way of utilizing the Shine theory). Showing interest in other people's content can help you too.

Use the Hashtag System

Just like Tik Tok, hashtags are an important part of Instagram. It is the middleman between you and the right audience. It's the lowest building block, especially when you're just starting out.

If you think using heaps of hashtags, including ones that do not correlate with your niche, will help, you might be wrong. It would be misusing the hashtag system, and that leads you to a direct road to the bad side of Instagram because they do, in fact, notice those who try abusing the algorithm. And not to mention, you are not gaining anything by trying to show it to people who have no interest in your niche.

The maximum quantity of hashtags you are allowed to use is 30 per post, and yes, use all those 30. Try writing those hashtags in the first comment rather than in the caption, so it looks a bit more well put together.

Perhaps not all hashtags that you assume are nice would be suitable for your own use. It is why every last one of you would want to verify to see whether the material is important to your subject.

When deciding whether a hashtag is right for your post, there are two key considerations to have a look at Niche and Dimension.

Never use only the most famous and vague hashtags, thinking you would be able to reach a larger crowd because you won't. You'll just be a hidden needle in a haystack. An invisible need at that. Why?

Because they aren't specific enough, and a lot of popular influencers already use those so you wouldn't be too noticed yet.

Please make sure you have certain hashtags that you use in every post (with fewer follows) so that you can be noticed by at least one familiar audience (needless to say, they need to be your target audience too).

It would be best if you would be able to find a middle ground between hashtags that not one soul has ever heard of before and hashtags that everyone knows about. Both would reward you little. Try hashtags that have about 90,000-900,000 post range.

Sorry, But Buying Is NOT the Way to Go

You can purchase double-taps or follows in due to despair just to see whether a lift is what they needed to get moving all along. But while this may make you appear popular to random people; it couldn't be farther from the facts.

Finally, they consider giving up both as a waste of time on Instagram and stop bringing in any considerable effort to expand, since they just do not see what else there is to do. Don't purchase likes, fans, and also, don't try the old trick of interaction pods.

Yes, even Instagram notices it if you buy followers/likes/views. Not only Instagram but also your followers. Which makes things a lot worse. And so, you won't gain any kind of income from that.

Using Highlights

Utilize the highlights feature and make/or find suitable cover photos for each to maintain consistency. It is making a profile that's pleasing to the eye and fitting for your niche and target audience.

4.4: Seeing is Believing

You may think this is all talk and no action, so let's drive that notion away by looking at a few of the many influencers on Instagram.

Notice the overall layout of this account. The username and profile instantly tell the users what the account is about.

Just the username would do this for us too but @wedarkacademia further described what it was about as well as threw in a bit of personality to the description as well as handles for other social platforms.

Their posts are consistent and related to one another. See the Highlights categorized neatly too.

@wedarkacademia Via Instagram

Responses like these encourage so much growth and engagement amongst the target audience.

@jonnajinton Via Instagram

@madeyemoodswing interacting with their audience. Their username being humorous and instantly getting the attention of Harry Potter fans who understand the reference.

Drawing in users of various kinds though if @madeyemoodswing doesn't involve any kind of Harry Potter related content, those fans may lose interest.

@madeyemoodswing Via Instagram

Jonna Jinton, blogging her art, photography and life on Instagram whilst also mentioning that she works on another platform (YouTube). Her posts are coherent and in sync with nature and mostly winter in her home country.

Her description and highlights are simple and straight to the point which a lot of users would find convenient and contemporary.

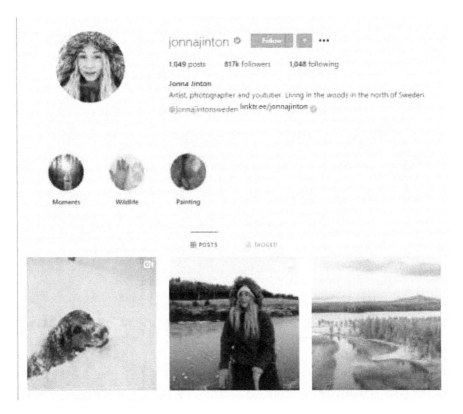

@jonnajinton Via Instagram

CHAPTER V: Ideas for Newbies

5.1: Idea Generation

There is not much to implement without ideas, and since the implementation is the secret to progress, creative ideas are required to enable some sort of change. It is clear that thoughts alone are not going to make creativity possible, since you need to be able to construct a structured mechanism to handle such innovations. The concept is not only about producing lots of it but also about bringing care to the nature of it.

It's not easy to create grade A content 24/7. Often people find it difficult to break out of their usual routine and habits when thinking about working on something new. In order to get out of the negative spiral, you need to glance at the development of creativity altogether and incorporate a few of the most key factors, strategies, and procedures that could be used more routinely to produce fresh concepts.

Perhaps you need original thoughts so a new possibility can be thoroughly explored?

Maybe you are trying to find a new way of solving a creativity barrier, or are you hoping for a decent answer to the dilemma?

Why does it matter?

Generating ideas is the outcome of creating complex, tangible, or conceptual theories. It's at the top of the funnel for concept organization, which works on seeking potential alternatives to true or suspected challenges and possibilities.

Ideas are, as stated, the very first move into change. Fresh theories rely on you progressing as independent individuals. From the point of view of a person, whether you feel stuck with a job or otherwise unable to resolve that one dilemma, fresh solutions will motivate you to push ahead.

The aim of fresh concepts is to reinforce the manner in which you work, irrespective of your priorities or the kinds of things you're searching for.

To fuel productivity and improve nature on a broader scale, societies rely on creativity. Creativity improves emerging innovations and enterprises. They are providing creators with more opportunities.

How do you do it?

Chances are, you brainstorm. However, it's been found that brainstorming requires more time and tends to fewer ideas as of planning, logging, and managing the meeting would take a lot more time than it should. While there are certain approaches to boost the quality of brainstorming, it's preferred if brainstorming isn't your first thought.

Nevertheless, certain methods are worth taking a look at. As you're searching for various kinds of ideas, it is beneficial to have methods in mind that help in developing them. Several of these concept development approaches may be used for further productive brainstorming and another creativity type.

5.2: The Techniques

Challenging proposals

This concept is when you bring an issue or opportunity into view due to the possibility of innovatively solving it. It can let you make a certain doubt about your content and aim it at your audience to get more ideas and useful opinions after you have identified what you intend to gain from it.

These idea challenges come in handy, especially when you're looking to engage a large audience of up to 10000. When you plan an idea challenge, pre-define the outcomes you'd like, the niche, followers, subscribers, etc. Make sure you keep track of the time with this technique to make sure it's working.

Similarities

You can use data and statistics from previous posts or videos on social media platforms to improve on ideas for another piece of content; this is thinking simultaneously. It is the simplest way of generating fresh content as it's often experimented with and succeeded.

In Example, YouTuber's making reaction videos continually but of various kinds of content.

SCAMPER

This method applies critical thinking to alter creativity, which is already present—adjusting open-source ideas to improve and agree on the best answer.

1. Substitution – Your old content being substituted with others to gain improvement.

2. Combining- Merging two or more ideas into one master idea for your content.

3. Adapting- Evaluates the options to make a method more versatile and works on the design, system, or principle alongside other related gradual changes.

4. Modification- From a broader context, changing not only the concept but also changing the concept looks at the challenge or potential and tries to change the outcomes.

5. Improvising by putting to another use- Searching for opportunities to use the concept or current content for some other reason and, if applicable to other areas of your profile or channel, analyzes the potential advantages.

6. Elimination- This technique studies all the possibilities, and if you find more than one fragment was removed.

7. Reversal- The emphasis of this procedure is to reverse the order of factors that can be swapped of your idea.

This technique was originated from the idea of brainstorming, but it applies to your thinking technique too. If you make generating ideas a daily activity by a series of trivial things, you could have a decent chance of winning the main breakthrough. Occasionally all it takes is really to reflect on what you already have. Sometimes, creators want to worry about the next remarkable thing being discovered. It is easy to overlook that the endless gradual changes are the aspects that can have a difference in the medium haul while creating fresh concepts. As a baseline, utilizing your existing theories or methods will explain a lot in relation to your present content, and that is what the SCAMPER strategy is really about.

Reverse Psychology

This method will make you challenge your content-related perceptions. Reverse thinking comes in handy when you feel you are trapped in the traditional mentality, and it appears to be impossible to come up with such unique ideas. It helps in checking our routinely-habits as the answer to finding more content isn't always a straight-to-the-point road. You consider the possibilities of what the opposite would do for your profile or channel, even if you end up thinking of the most peculiar of solutions.

5.3: Once You've Got It

Organizing Ideas

Once you've got all those ideas down, planning and organizing them can be difficult if you don't know where to start. Creators need to collect this creativity as soon as it comes to them instead of using it as soon as it comes up.

Jotting down all your ideas in a notebook or on your phone can be helpful, and most people do this as it's only for personal use. But if you wish for other people's opinions on the matter to know their judgment, this could be a hassle. Not to worry though, there are things like idea management tools to aid you with that.

Management

A concept tool for effective functions as the foundation of the method of idea planning. This is how you can assemble the ideas, analyze them, debate, prioritize them, take account of their success, and the overall course of the operations of your idea generation.

Since concept planning is such a huge subject and famous influencers or public figures are likely to have loads of suggestions, it often makes perfect sense for most influencers or creators to use a designated idea management system.

It is just as productive to handle ideas with a designated method as the underlying mechanism at the back end. You could create a mechanism that makes it a lot easier to produce and refine fresh concepts and create ideas a persistent practice. The methods that are too confusing can infuriate people, so try not to make things too difficult.

5.4: Winning at Creativity

The Appropriate Crowd

It is necessary to include the right individuals in the equation for the content to be as efficient as possible. Start engaging all influencers who know about the content creation and are sincerely involved in you making a difference.

Ensure your community is the target audience and well educated on the topic if the aim is to involve a wider community of users to produce ideas.

Determine Your Objective

Aim to collect as much relevant data as possible about the content you wish to make before you begin to understand the source. Define what you understand about it by now and what data is still required.

Though it sounds simple, the further you can clearly explain your actual idea, the greater the odds of producing practical ideas are.

Limits to Keep an Eye Out For.

It can impede imagination to convey that every idea is a valid idea, so ensure the aims are ambitious and precise enough. One approach to get some of the viewers' genuinely innovative thoughts is to set limits.

If the ultimate aim is to cut prices, suggestions such as investing truly little on content would certainly come to mind when you want to save up. The thoughts you get, though, would vary greatly if you ask yourself: "How could I save 50% on expenses and create unique and engaging content?".

Deduction

The goal of creating original approaches is to improve what is already present as well as to produce something new.

From a different angle, coming up with entirely novel solutions will help you tackle your creativity block. It helps you to widen the spectrum of thoughts beyond the present style of learning, which inevitably leads to much more ideas.

Sometimes, creators, influencers, and public figures use current ideas or behavioral templates while attempting to get started on a social media platform instead of attempting to think of the latest ideas. The concern with this technique is that it does not encourage you to pursue multiple options and limits the number of possibilities.

5.5: About Yourself

Who are you?

Create a clip of yourself being introduced. Who are you, what are you doing? On your YouTube channel, Tik Tok, or Instagram profile, what should viewers hope to see? How frequently do you upload photos or videos? Create videos to let them know exactly what they should expect, inviting viewers to your channel or page. Aim to give a convincing argument for audiences to click on the subscribe button on YouTube and follow on Instagram or Tik Tok.

Vlogging

Making Vlogs can be informative, fun, intimate, anything you would like to create of it, much like traditional writing. Almost all influencers and public figures may use material from vlogs to involve fans and expand their communities.

A Day in Your Life

YouTubers love to walk through The Day in your Life videos from another's perspective. Once you wake up the next morning and lead audiences to a normal day in your schedule, start filming.

Matt D'Avella Via YouTube

Behind-the-curtain Content

Showcase to the viewers what's going on at the back end of your Instagram account, YouTube channel, or Tik Tok account. With this famous video style, let your audience see behind the curtains. You can display your room, your house, your workplace, your city, anywhere else you enjoy.

20 Questions

You could make short clips or long clips (depending on your preference or niche) playing a game of 20 questions. These questions can be personal or silly, and the best have a little bit of both. Letting your audience be closer to you is what this accomplishes.

'Draw My Life.'

These kinds of videos are often found on YouTube, where the creator essentially draws their life often on a whiteboard with stick figures and narrating their life so far. Of course, you decide how much or how little you wish to say about yourself. Majority 'Draw my life' videos include key events or milestones in their lives.

You can even introduce your family, background, and friends in these.

5.6: Trending Content Ideas

Teach them How to Cook (or how not to)

This kind of content is often made by entertainment-focused or cooking influencers. You can make it an A grade cooking tutorial, or you could completely twist it depending on your creativity and teach people how not to cook but let them have an enjoyable time watching creators do it wrong.

For example, YouTuber 'Simply Nailogical' made a video called 'Baking a cake with Nail Polish' on 18th September 2016, which got over 5 Million views. The cake was quite inedible but still entertaining to watch to over 5 Million people.

You can make this an Instagram post, a Tik-Tok video, or a YouTube video.

Workout Routine

As it's time to start working out, lots of folks look towards YouTube videos, quick Tik Tok hacks, or Instagram posts/IGTV videos for specific fitness routines, as well as how to do those workouts. Both common subjects are exercise, stretching, or shape footage.

Understanding the Complicated Mess

Informative and aurally captivating means of presenting data and figures that could otherwise be dull or difficult to grasp is infographics related content. Content that helps your audience's day a little easier. Every genre of content has specific things that not everyone understands, so try finding the most commonly found problem in yours and present content on that!

Reviewing other People's Products

One of the most common kinds of information on these social media platforms is product reviews. Before deciding to buy, thousands of viewers check out this insightful content. Tech gadgets and make-up items are common themes, but reviews can be sought for all types of goods.

For example, YouTuber Marques Brownlee's Niche is tech gadgets, and a majority, maybe even all, of his video's reviews on really expensive gadgets so often people who think about buying a new phone or the PS5 watch his videos to see his opinion on it. His video called 'PlayStation 5 Review: NextGen Gaming!' received almost 6 Million views!

You can make review videos on any and every genre of content! Games, movies, books, food, universities, perfumes, songs, shows, even countries! So, search for things you can review in your niche.

Comedy Videos

In the event that you need to turn into a web sensation, an entertaining video may very well assist you with getting there. A sizable number of the most mainstream recordings on YouTube, Instagram, and Tik Tok ended up in such a state since this sort of content made watchers chuckle or laugh.

Pranks

Viewers love watching tricks. Pull a trick on somebody (innocuous tricks, please) and share the outcomes on your social media platforms.

Tricks have not been altogether contemplated; however, scientists have discovered that individuals find being deceived an extremely aversive encounter. Trick based humor can be coldblooded or kind, cherished or detested; however, it's not straightforward.

Furry Creatures Content

Dogs, little cats, child elephants, the Internet loves charming/interesting creature recordings are considerably more popular than recordings of human children. So, if you have a pet, share it with the world! Everyone loves animals.

Music Videos

Singing a song cover, and original, or even lip-syncing is always a fun sight to see. Indeed, even late-night TV gets in on the good times. Pick a mainstream tune and give it a shot!

If you have a bad voice, don't worry; try making it hilarious by a funny parody where you impress the audience with clever and witty lyrics rather than your vocals.

Fact Check

What are some myths that are commonly believed by the vast majority regarding your niche? Compile all the misconceptions and make a post or video on the matter. Show emotion and teach your audience the stereotypes believed about your niche by the public.

As the internet is filled with so much information, a fair share of it is fake news, so spreading awareness about it would be intriguing for your audience (as long as you stay on topic).

Often people are found spreading rumors without even knowing they are rumors and not facts, so content that addresses the rumors is an interesting concept for anyone.

Needless to say, double-check whether the information you are giving your audience is proven with evidence to be right. Or else those mistakes can decrease your followers/subscribers quick.

Write a catchy caption or thumbnail with a question that quickly catches their interest. For example, '10 Myths you probably believed about professional cooks' or '6 reasons why you should not believe every thing you're told'.

Speed-run

Can you play games as fast as humanely possible? Finish your make-up in under 2 minutes? Or maybe you can make a 3-course meal in under an hour? Show off those skills on social media!

Speed-runs are commonly found on gaming channels so viewers can quickly experience a gameplay without having to play it themselves due to the cost of the game or less time of time.

Time-slip

@jonnajinton Via Instagram on April 17th , 2020

Time-lapse is a method where the casings of the video are caught at a far slower speed than expected. Traffic, mists, and the sunrise all will, in general, be well-known time-slip by subjects. The outcome is frequently hypnotizing.

Some creators make time-lapses of their artwork to show progress quickly as an art piece can take at least a few hours.

Shopping/Mail Hauls

This type of video is particularly well known with style vloggers and beauty. After an outing to the shopping center, flaunt your take piece by piece. From the freshest iPhone to an in-vogue membership box or the most trending toy, individuals love to watch others open boxes. So next time you do another package, don't simply tear into it; make sure you are recording first!

You could even give out your address and your audience would send you mail. Often YouTubers make mail opening videos reviewing all the heartfelt gifts their watchers send them.

Go Live

Why trust that the recap will show individuals what's happened? Take your watchers to the occasion with you by live-streaming to your Instagram Live, Tik Tok Live, or YouTube Live. Even after the session is over, the stream would still be accessible online.

You can schedule a certain day for every week in which you go live and make sure you let everyone know through all your social media platforms, so they are aware and wait for you to go live.

What Most Do

A substantial number of the top Instagrammers are singers, sports brands, actors, footballers, models, and of course, Instagram themselves. The most famous YouTuber channels are often among the genre of trailer channels, singers, gamers, kids show, hack tutorial channels, and so on. Tik Tokers are often found to be comedians, musicians, artists, etc.

The best content? Ones that are so good that people feel the need to see it on other platforms too, Tik Tok video compilations on YouTube, and Tik Tok videos on Instagram, Live videos on Instagram recorded and put-on YouTube. The type of content that is put across various platforms are the ones that have gone viral or loved enough that users wish to see it almost everywhere.

Conclusion

First things first, it would be beneficial if you ask yourself, what do you have to offer? Why would people want to watch your videos? What are they getting out of the time they spent on your video?

Is it educational? Hilarious? Scary? Relaxing? Silly? Helpful? Inspiring or motivational? Perhaps very random, either way, would your target audience enjoy or show any interest in it?

Maintain originality- the charm of social media is that you can express your thoughts and add a little more to *you*, so to speak. You can grow on YouTube, Tik Tok, and Instagram, only if you have something no one else has to give out. The basic rule to starting a business, 'what's so special about you?' or 'what do you have that no one else does?'. Write down all that comes to mind when answering these questions.

You can not copy peoples' ideas, only your own significant expression of those ideas into your videos, posts, stories, etc. However, if your content seems to be matching someone else's a little too much, change it up, brainstorm a little about what you could do to make it unique, and choose the best one. And be certain you aren't tuning out any other possibilities due to your fears.

Honesty- be honest about your opinions and where you stand. This can be a random video about car reviews or your opinion on white supremacy; it need not matter. Maybe you feel like changing your genre after a long time, but you're afraid of losing the number of followers/subscribers you've gotten so far. Your fear is valid, but you can't force yourself to put out content on something you have no more interest in anymore because you followers/subscriber will notice eventually, and they'll just fade out on their own. So, try being honest, raw, and authentic from the start.

However, being honest does not amount to being insensitive. You're trying to be the person people look up to or look forward to viewing when they're having a difficult day, so try to fill those expectations without disregarding your bad days, of course. Ending things on a positive note and be accepting of the honest truth your followers/subscribers/viewers offer in return.

Humility- Try not to overthink each comment they make because what seems like an hour of thought to you was probably not more than five minutes to them. When you start noticing your growth, don't become egotistic about it, or the people that put you where you are today will leave as fast as they came. Nobody likes a showoff.

Setting boundaries- deciding where you draw the line between your public and personal life is vital. You don't need to broadcast every minute detail about your personal life to the entire world, and you need to value the privacy of the people close to you if you wish for the same.

Motivation- find that mechanism that triggers, leads, and retains your aiming habits. Whether it be intrinsic or extrinsic motivation, keep a daily reminder for it, so you keep that drive and motivation to continue working hard. Grabbing a coffee, chocolate bar, reading, or some inspirational quote is what puts you in a nice mood and sparks wisdom, do it every day.

The physical, internal, cultural, and mental factors which trigger action are involved in motivation. Introjected motivation is when you are driven to work out of the guilt of procrastination or laziness. Identified motivation is when you know you have got work to do, yet you haven't determined anything in regard to it. Try to avoid introjected and identified motivation as it originates from a negative space.

Don't give up if you feel like you are not getting enough growth, stay consistent and keep at it no matter what. If you still feel like there has been no effect, try going over the points again and make sure you keep track of how you have been doing by statistically analyzing yourself.

Soon enough, you will catch yourself with 10,000 followers/subscribers on YouTube, Instagram, and Tik Tok. It is more or less a smooth ride from there. Good Luck!

The 9+1 Best Home-Based Business Model of 2021

Find Out how Millennials Have Built Millionaire Businesses from Home with Soap and Candle Making, Natural Cosmetics and much more

By

Nespy Online Marketing

Table of Contents

Introduction

Karsanbhai Patel (Patel), the chemist at Mines and Geology Department of the Gujarat Government, produced synthetic powder of detergent phosphate-free in 1969 and began selling this locally. He priced the new yellow powder at 3.50rs per kg. It was at one time when Rs 15 was being charged for Hindustan Lever Limited (HLL) Surf. Soon, in Kishnapur (Gujarat), Patel's hometown, there was a big demand for Nirma. In 10x12 feet space in his home, he began preparing the formula. He had named powder after his daughter's name-Nirupama. On the way to the office by bicycle, about 15 kilometers away, Patel was able to sell around 15-20 packets a day. Thus, the new journey began. Hindustan Lever Limited (HLL) responded in a manner characteristic of many global corporations in the early 1970s, when washing powder Nirma was launched into the market of low-income. "That isn't our business," senior executives said of the new offering. "We don't have to be worried." However very soon, Hindustan Lever Limited (HLL) was persuaded by Nirma's performance in the detergent sector that this wanted to take a closer gaze at the less income market. Low-cost detergents & toilet soaps are almost synonymous with the brand name. Nirma, on the other hand, found that it would've to launch goods targeted at the higher end of the market to maintain the middle-class buyers as they moved up the market. For the luxury market, the firm introduced bathroom soaps. Analysts, on the other hand, claimed Nirma wouldn't be capable of duplicate its performance in the premium market. In the year 2000, the Nirma had a 15 percent share of the toilet soap market and a 30% share of the detergent market. Nirma's revenue for the year ended in March 2000 grew by 17 percent over the previous fiscal year, to 17.17rs. bn, backed by volume development and commissioning of backward integration projects. By 1985, in many areas of the world, washing powder Nirma became one of the most common detergent brands. Nirma was a global consumer company by 1999, with a wide variety of soaps, detergents, & personal care items. Nirma has brought in the latest technologies for the manufacturing facilities in six locations across India, in line with its ideology of delivering premium goods at the best possible costs. The success of Nirma in the intensely competitive market for soaps & detergents was due to its efforts to support the brand, which had been complemented by the sales scope & market penetration. The network of Nirma spread across the country, with over two million outlets of retail and 400 distributors. Nirma was able to reach out to even the smallest villages due to its vast network. Nirma spread to the markets overseas in 1999 after establishing itself in India. Via a joint venture called Commerces Overseas Limited, it made its first foray into Bangladesh. Within a year, the company had risen to the top of Bangladesh's detergent market. Other areas such as Middle East, Russia, China, Africa & additional Asian countries were also intended for the entry of the organization. Nirma became a 17 billion Rs company in 3 decades, beginning as a single-product single-man article of clothing in 1969. Under the umbrella name Nirma, the company had several production plants and a large product range. The mission of the organization to have "Better Product, Better Values and Better Living" added much to its growth. Nirma was able to outshine Hindustan Levers Limited (then HLL) and carve out a niche for oneself in the lower-ends of detergent & market toilet soap. HLL's Surf was the first to be used as a detergent powder in India in 1959. But by the 1970s, merely by making the product available at a reasonable price, Nirma led the demand for detergent powder. Nirma launched its Nirma Beauty soaps to the Indian toilet soap industry in 1990. Nirma had gained a 15% share of 530,000 tons per annum toilet soap industry by 1999, making it India's second-largest producer. Although it was way behind HLL's 65 percent share, the success of Nirma was impressive compared to Godrej, which had an 8 percent share. By 1999-2000, Nirma had already acquired a 38 percent share of India's detergent market of 2.4 million tonnes. For the same period, HLL's market share was 31%. In this book, we will study and analyze the case of Nirma and its rise to the top detergent companies of India. Besides, we will also give profitable ideas and options for starting a lucrative detergent soap, candle making, and natural cosmetics business.

CHAPTER 1: The Nirma Washing Powder's Success Story

The success story of the famous Nirma washing powder began in a small Gujarati farmer's house. We'll tell you about a billionaire father who lost his daughter in a car crash and later discovered a way to get her back to life. When she was alive, only a few people knew of her daughter, but it was the sheer persistence and willpower of this man that made his daughter famous in the world, even though she was no more. This is the story of a man who was born into a poor farming family and turned his daughter's nickname into India's leading detergent, soda ash, and education brand. A man of valor and passion who showed that nothing will hinder you if you have the willpower. Here is the story of **"Sabki Pasand Nirma, Washing Powder Nirma."**

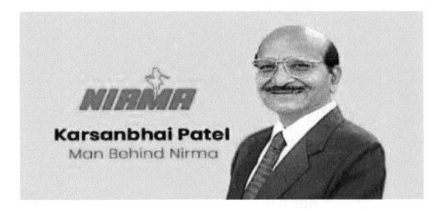

1.1 Invention of Nirma detergent?

Karsanbhai was born in Ruppur, Gujarat, to a farmer's family in 1945. He had earned a bachelor's degree in chemistry by the age of 21. He attempted to do a normal job like his colleagues at first. He served as a lab technician for the Lalbhai Group's New Cotton Mills, which is credited with launching the Indian jeans movement. He also took up a position at the Geology and Mining Department of the Gujarat government after this short stint. The year 1969 marked the start of a turning point in the career trajectory of Karsanbhai. It was at this time that Hindustan Lever Ltd (now Hindustan Unilever) formed a full monopoly on the Indian detergent market under the brand name "Surf." A Surf Pack was sold somewhere from Rs 10-15 back then. The USP was that, unlike normal washing soap bars, it eliminated stains from your clothes and didn't irritate your skin. However, for middle-class families, which had no other choice than to return to the old bar soap, this price point was not affordable. The tycoon in Karsanbhai noticed the issue and devised a plan. A young Karsanbhai will come home from work and dedicate all his time and energy to making a phosphate-free detergent in his yard. He wanted to bear in mind that he needed to produce a detergent with a low manufacturing cost so that everybody could afford it. Karsanbhai utilized a recipe for a yellow-colored detergent powder that could be marketed for a mere Rs 3 after several trials and failures. He chose to name the invention after Nirupama, his daughter. He finally got the formula right one day, and as an after-work business, he began making detergents in his 100-square-foot backyard. He will cycle around the neighborhoods, selling door-to-door homemade detergent packages. Patel set the price of his detergent at Rs. 3, almost a third less than Hindustan Unilever's well-known brand "Surf." The product's high quality and low price made it a success, and it was well-received by many who saw great benefit in purchasing it. Because of the business's high promise, Karsanbhai quit his government job three years later to pursue it full-time. Karsanbhai was so fond of the commodity that he called it Nirma, after his daughter Nirupama's nickname. To make sure that everybody remembers her, he used her picture (the girl in the white frock) on the pack and in TV advertisements. Such was a father's love for his daughter. While Karsanbhai Patel himself was not an MBA graduate, the techniques he adopted to expand his company left marketers bewildered and amazed. 'Nirma' was not only a game-changer but also a trendsetter for several small companies. Here are a couple of 'Washing Powder Nirma's' management lessons.

1.2 Karsanbhai Patel's sale policy for Nirma detergent

Karsanbhai Patel agreed to start marketing it once the product had a strong formula. On his cycle, he used to go door-to-door and neighborhood-to-neighborhood every day for three years, pitching the detergent. As it was a brand new product, if they found the product poor, he gave his consumers a money-back guarantee. Nirma has been the cheapest detergent in Ahmedabad at the time. As a result, Karsanbhai's product was an immediate hit. He left his government job three years later and set up a store in Ahmedabad to carry out this full-time enterprise. In some areas of Gujarat, his brand was doing very well, but there was a need to expand its scope. At the time, the standard was to offer the product to retailers on credit. This was a huge gamble because if the product didn't sell, Karsanbhai would have had to close down the company. At that time, he chose to try something different. He planned to spend a little money on advertising. These commercials, with their catchy jingles, were directed at housewives. And this bet paid off well. Nirma became a famous household brand and it had to be purchased by people. He did, however, remove 90% of the stock from the market at this time. Potential buyers had asked for the detergent at their local retailers for about a full month but would have to return empty-handed. During this time, retail store owners flocked to Karsanbhai, demanding that the detergent supply be increased. After another month, he eventually decided. Nirma was able to take over the sales and even beat Surf at their own game due to this approach. It went on to become the country's highest-selling detergent. It remained India's largest-selling detergent even after a decade,

1.3 Invest In Research and Development

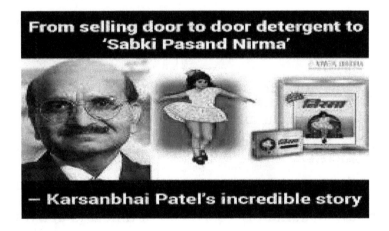

Karsanbhai Patel had little means and was not a man born with a silver spoon in his mouth. Karsanbhai loved experimenting with chemicals after completing a B.Sc. in Chemistry at the age of 21 and then working as a laboratory technician. He noticed that only MNCs in India were selling detergents and there was no economy brand detergent for the country. His excitement about bridging the distance grew, sensing a massive opening, and Karsanbhai began experimenting with chemicals. He quickly succeeded in manufacturing a detergent of high quality at a much cheaper price, which was an immediate success in the industry. Every good product needs a substantial expenditure in time, resources, and commitment in research and development.

1.4 No Higher Costs

Nirma had rewritten the rules of the game within a short time, by delivering high-quality goods at an unprecedentedly low price. Nirma's success was due to its cost-cutting policy. Patel had concentrated from the very beginning on delivering high-value goods at the lowest price possible. The corporation sought to keep improving efficiency while reducing prices. Nirma sought out captive processing plants for raw materials to keep production costs to a minimum. This led to the backward integration initiative, as part of which, at Baroda and Bhavnagar, which became operational in 2000, two state-of-the-art plants were established. This also led to a reduction in raw-material prices. Ahead of time and at a much smaller cost than anticipated, the two new plants were completed. The Baroda plant's second phase was finished 6 months ahead of schedule and at a cost of Rs.2.5 billion compared to the initial projected cost of Rs. 2.8 billion. Compared to the initial projected cost of Rs. 10.36 billion, the Bhavnagar plant was finished in a record period of 2 years at a cost of

Rs.9.86 billion. This plant had a workforce of just 500 employees. Concerning Nirma's plant, Tata Chemical's plant, which had around twice the amount, employed ten times the number of workers. Almost 65000 tpa of N-Paraffin was produced by the Baroda plant for Linear Alkyl Benzene (LAB) and Synthetic detergents. Similarly, almost 4.20,000 tpa of soda ash could be produced by the Bhavnagar facility. Akzo Nobel Engineering in Holland produced the Akzo Dry Lime technology used in this factory. The plant had 108 kilometers of salt bunds, which would assist in the potential development of vacuum iodized salt. Patel said, "We have a processing potential of three lakh tons of pure salt. No one in the world had a related plant, but Tata Salt." Nirma had reduced its distribution costs by obviating the need for middlemen. The item went to the dealer straight from the manufacturer. Hiren K Patel (Hiren), CMD, explained to Nirma Customer Care Ltd., "An order is placed and the truck immediately leaves. It's similar to a bank account. We're sending stock, they're sending money." In states like Tamil Nadu, Andhra Pradesh, and southern Karnataka, the company-maintained depots, as it was often difficult to bring stocks to these regions. Stocks were shipped directly from the plants in states like Madhya Pradesh and Uttar Pradesh. In March 2000, Nirma opted for in-house packaging and printing by obtaining Kisan Factories at Moriya, near Ahmedabad, in a further cost-cutting exercise. Nirma hoped that this would increase the packaging's quality.

1.5 Be Proactive in your approach as it is beneficial for the business

Karsanbhai Patel was the only person who started this business and starting selling Nirma. He was educated and had a government career, but he was never afraid of selling door-to-door detergent. He was diligent in doing something and knew that the company was tiny and bootstrapping, so he had to consider everything and anything about his business that could be fruitful. There is no such thing as a small or large undertaking. And if you are the CEO, you should embrace the obligations that are valuable to the company without guilt.

1.6 Provide Customers with 'Value for Money'

Customers noticed the advantages of purchasing Nirma, and it became an immediate success. They considered the standard to be at par with the giant Surf brand, but to take advantage of the same perks, they just had to pay one-third of the amount. Customers would only appreciate the product if you show them the advantages and give them decent value for their money.

1.7 Define Your Segment

Karsanbhai Patel identified the target segment for his detergent almost as soon as he found the magical formula. He realized that a luxury brand sold in tier 1 cities was the alternative Surf brand, so he concentrated on marketing his brand in tier 2-3 cities. He priced his detergent low and made it a mass brand to get more consumer traction. People from the lower middle class and middle class quickly adopted the product, and it quickly rose in popularity. Where most firms adopted the conventional top-down strategy, i.e., spreading from metro towns to rural cities, Nirma did the reverse and changed the whole game. It is really important to evaluate the competitors for every company and define the most lucrative segment.

1.8 Focus on Building a Brand

It was failing to find vendors outside the city in the early 80s, although the commodity was approved on a small scale in Ahmedabad. Since clients were unaware of its presence, retailers were wary of keeping the detergent in their stores. It resulted in overdue payments, return on inventory, and large business losses. Karsanbhai

Patel came up with a good publicity approach to handle the situation and launched a TV advertisement campaign. The popular "Washing powder Nirma, detergent tikiya Nirma" jingle became an anthem for the company and customers began to equate Nirma as a strong brand. The demand for Nirma soon peaked, and with his products, Patel flooded the retail stores. A good brand decreases a buyer's potential risk and increases the company's bargaining power.

1.9 Astutely Manage the Brand Wars

Nirma also had innovative marketing campaigns. Nirma successfully spread the name to other product segments in the mid-nineties, such as premium detergents (Nirma Mega Detergent Cake and Washing Powder), premium toilet soaps, and (Nirma Sandal, Nima Premium, Nirma Lime Fresh). In both the economy and luxury markets, it maintained its initial pricing and marketing plans. In 2000, with Nirma Beauty Shampoo, Nirma Shikakai, and Toothpaste, the firm entered the hair care market. Soaps, unlike detergents, were a private-care commodity. Many consumers had strong emotional attachments with their soap products. Furthermore, HLL segmented the market by price, fragrance appeal, and brand personality. So, against Lifebuoy, Nirma put Nirma Wash, Nirma Beauty Soap against Lux, Nima Rose against Breeze7, and Nima Lime against Jai Lime. Explaining how Nirma hoped to win this match, playing by the rules of HLL, Hiren said"Worldwide, there are only four or five channels that account for most of the soaps sold: floral, fashion, fitness, freshness." With the relevant scents, Nirma manufactured high-fatty-matter soaps and priced them much lower than other brands. As a result, the 'sub-premium' section was born. The game of controlling the geographical variety of market desires was also perfected by Nirma. The North, for instance, favored pink soaps, and green ones were favored by the South. In the South, sandal soaps were more common. Initially, the company's promotional budget, relative to other FMCG firms, was very poor. In contrast to the usual 6-10 percent, Nirma spent just 1.25-2 percent of its sales on ads. The firm used starlets such as Sangeeta Bijlani, Sonali Bendre, and Riya Sen, who were comparatively unknown at the time, to endorse soaps. The promotional messages were both transparent and centered on the product's benefits. Nirma still chose to first put the item on the shelf, get reviews, and then create a lasting ad campaign. Nirma used its tried-and-true tool, price, to introduce toilet soaps and detergents in the premium market. In these divisions, the company intended to rely on quantities as well. However, the margins granted to retailers had shifted. Unlike economic goods, where the cost advantages were passed on to customers, this advantage was passed on to retailers by Nirma. It provided them with massive profit margins. For instance, it offered 52 percent for Nirma premium soap and an incredible margin of 140 percent for Nirma shampoo. In the luxury segment of the soap industry, observers were pessimistic about Nirma's chances of success.

Unlike detergents, the demand for soaps and shampoos was incredibly fragmented. There were only 15-20 brands, and it was hard to get a considerable market share for any soap. This market was also less price sensitive. So, it was hard for any enterprise to support itself on price alone. Analysts thought that shifting the brand value of Nirma would take years. According to a survey conducted by Nirma's marketing agency, Samsika Marketing Consultancy, Nirma was viewed as a low-cost brand. Many people were almost afraid to say they used it. Nirma published corporate advertisements worth Rs 10 bn in India in the late nineties to shed this image. Analysts claim that the fast-growing shampoo market is a safer investment than luxury soaps. Just 30% of the population in India used shampoo, with more than 70% of this group living in urban areas. However, according to some researchers, while the rural market's presumed potential was very high, it was difficult to convince rural folk to use shampoos in actual practice. A further concern faced by Nirma was that of insufficient facilities. While it had a good presence in the smaller towns and villages, it lacked the requisite network for urban centers to penetrate. As a result, Nirma's foray into high-end soaps and shampoos proved to be a flop.

1.10 Diversify the Portfolio

For low-income groups, Nirma began with a low-cost detergent, but later introduced products for higher-income groups, such as Nirma Sandal soap, Nirma Beauty soap, etc.

Not just that, but in 2003, Karsanbhai Patel formed Nirma University to diversify the company's brand portfolio. The brand is currently exploring its options in the cement industry to grow its market. Diversifying the portfolio decreases the company's potential risk of loss while still allowing it to serve a broader variety of consumers.

1.11 Conclusion

While Nirma was best known as a manufacturer of goods for the low-cost economy, it was popular in the middle and upmarket segments. Yet rivalry was also growing at the same time. Although HLL continued to be a major threat, offensive initiatives were also introduced by P&G and Henkel SPIC. In the detergent and washing powder market, participants from the unorganized field were also introduced to the rivalry. Patel was confident of tackling the rivalry, though. "He added, "We keep the price line and the happy customer returns to us normally. Based on its growth strategy, the company has risen in demand and volume in the last three decades: "A buyer is not looking for one-time frills or feel-good variables. The landlord, on the other hand, is searching for a long-term solution to his or her issues." Karsanbhai Patel, who began with a vision of making his daughter famous through his brand and ended up being one of the greatest entrepreneurs of all time, exemplifies the relevance of this quotation. He began with an aim of creating his daughter famous through his brand and ended up becoming one of the greatest entrepreneurs of all time. His name not only gained tremendous respect but also became a trendsetter for many new firms. The brand has taught young entrepreneurs many useful lessons and has proven to be a valuable resource for the region. Karsanbhai Patel has shown that no goal is too lofty if you have the ambition and zeal to achieve it.

1.12 What Karsanbhai Patel and Nirma detergent did for the Indian Economy

Nirma's meteoric growth in prominence culminated in the introduction of a new economic market for detergent powder. It was of good quality and was inexpensive. Plus, contrary to the others, the fact that it was manufactured without phosphates made it the most environmentally-friendly detergent. In comparison, a labor-consuming process was the process of producing the detergent. And thus, Nirma went on to hire more than 14,000 workers and became the country's leading employer.

1.13 Karsanbhai Patel's ventures other than the Nirma detergent

Karsanbhai wanted to grow his FMCG business after Nirma dominated the detergent industry. Nirma launched its line of toilet soaps, beauty soaps, and even shampoos in the premium market. While the latter venture failed, one of their products, edible salt Shudh, is still available and doing well. Overall, Nirma has a 20 percent market share in soap cakes and a 35 percent market share in detergents. That isn't it, however. In 1995, Karsanbhai Patel founded the Nirma Institute of Technology in Ahmedabad. Later, it became one of Gujarat's most prestigious engineering schools. After that, the whole structure was merged under the Nirma University of Science and Technology, which is supervised by the Nirma Education and Research Foundation, and in 2003, the entire structure was unified under the Nirma University of Science and Technology. This is overseen by the Nirma Education and Research Foundation. Since 2004, Karsanbhai's CSR initiative, Nirmalabs education, has aimed to train and incubate entrepreneurs. Karsanbhai Patel has now turned over the reins of his profitable company to his two sons. Pratibha Patil, the then-President of India, bestowed the Padma Shri on him in 2010. Nirma is now the world's biggest manufacturer of soda ash, and the company has been privately owned since 2012. Karsanbhai Patel invested his huge fortune on a six-seat chopper in 2013, which cost Rs 40 crore. After Gautam Adani (Adani Group) and Pankaj Patel (Zydus Group), he became the third Ahmedabad-based industrialist to purchase a helicopter. Nirma, on the other hand, is still one of India's most popular detergents. And the jingles will live on forever.

CHAPTER 2: Start a Profitable Soap Making Business

As a soap manufacturer, you'll create your recipes for soaps and probably other personal cleaning and beauty products. Ecommerce, farmers markets, arts events, wholesale positioning in spas and boutiques, and even door-to-door sales are all options for selling the goods. You'll test several solutions and see if you can find a steady stream of clients. Learn how to launch a soap-making company of your own.

Steps for starting a soap making business

You've uncovered the ideal market opportunity and are now prepared to take the next step. There's more to launching a company than simply filing papers with the government. We've put together a list of steps to help you get started with your soap-making business.

These measures will ensure that the new company is well-planned, legally compliant, and properly registered.

Plan your business

As an entrepreneur, you must have a well-thought-out strategy. It will assist you in figuring out the additional data of your organization and uncovering any unknowns. Given below are some key points to consider:

What are the startup and recurring costs?

Who is the targeted audience?

What is the maximum price you will charge from the customers?

What would you name your company?

What are the costs involved in opening a soap-making business?

You've got a good start if you have a kitchen or workspace as well as a few simple kitchen utensils. Making soap isn't an expensive business to undertake, but you would need to invest in some basic equipment. Ingredients cost at least $200. Lye and fats or oils are used to make soap. That's a good start, but it'll be your special formula that sets you apart. For superior feel, fragrance, and lather, you can use coconut oil, olive oil, almond oil, and several fragrance oils, extracts, and natural additives. To keep materials costs down and simplify production, you could start with only one or two simple recipes. Equipment for producing soap will cost around $300. Your equipment specifications will be determined by the type of soap-making you do.

Hot process, cold process, rebatching, and melt and pour are the four basic forms of processing, and each needs different equipment. But, regardless of the route you take, you'll almost definitely need soap molds, packing, and shipping items. You can get your basic ingredients, additives, equipment, and supplies from several online retailers. Marketing software will cost up to $750. A professional-looking website with enticing product images is key to the company's growth. Since your online consumers can't touch or smell your goods, they must be able to judge the good quality of what they see. That means recruiting a graphic designer and web developer to help you make the best out of your logo and online presence is a smart investment. To express your love and dedication to product quality, your visual imagery will be carried through in your labeling and branding. Skilled services will cost up to $200. Is it legal in your state and society for you to run this sort of business from home? Before you put up your shingle, meet with a lawyer for a quick consultation. The Handcrafted Soap & Cosmetics Guild charges a membership fee of $100 per year (HSCG). Small-batch soap makers will benefit from this organization's preparation, funding, and useful networking opportunities. Insurance for general liability and product liability would cost $265-$375 a year. This is also accessible via the HSCG.

What are the ongoing expenses for a soap-making business?

The consumable commodity materials you'll need for ongoing development would be your greatest ongoing expense. Your increasing variable expenses would be more than offset by a rise in revenue if you've priced your offering correctly.

Who is the target market?

While women make up the majority of the demand for homemade soaps, some firms have had success selling male-oriented soap scents. You may approach consumers who admire your product's consistency and luxury, or those who only purchase organic or vegan goods. Customers will note the difference in quality among your soaps and those sold on the shelves of a traditional supermarket.

How does a soap-making business make money?

In the majority of the cases, all of your revenue shall be derived from the products you make or sell.

How much can you charge customers?

Your goods could be sold for $5 or $6 a bar. This is more than your consumers are likely to spend for mass-produced retail soaps, but your product has a high perceived value. Other price points can be met by providing discounts on multiple orders, marketing multi-bar bundles, and extending the product range. Look at local rivals' websites to see what they're costing and how that would impact the pricing. Will you charge more to suggest a higher-end product range, or will you charge less to compensate for the lower per-unit sales margin with higher volume?

How much profit can a soap-making business make?

There are a few well-known soap makers who began their careers in the same way you did. Take, for example, Burt's Bees. Others in your business run it as a side venture, something between a crafts hobby and a modestly profitable business. You will go as far as your dedication, imagination, promotional skills, and hard work can take you, as with many home-based companies.

How can you make your business more profitable?

Many soap makers diversify their product range to include more exotic soaps (goat's milk soap is one example) or complementary goods. Making candles is a natural progression for soap makers who still use a hot process. Others are involved in home fragrances, lip balms, hair care, and even pet products. Focus on what else will cater to the consumer base when speaking about expanding your product mix. Many companies aim to maximize their net income by lowering the cost of goods produced. Growing the earnings by issuing bigger batches at a time is a cost-effective technique.

2.1 What will you name your business?

Choosing the correct name is vital and daunting. If you own a sole proprietorship, you should start using a separate company name from your own. We suggest reviewing the following references before filing a company name:

The state's business records

Federal and state trademark records

Social media sites

Web domain availability

It's important to have your domain name registered before anyone else does.

2.2 Form a legal entity

The sole proprietorship, partnership, limited liability company (LLC), and corporation are the most traditional corporate structures. If your soap manufacturing company is used, creating a legitimate business entity such as an LLC or corporation prevents you from being found legally accountable.

Register for taxes

Before you can start doing business, you'll need to apply for several state and federal taxes. You would need to apply for an EIN to pay for taxation. It's very basic and free.

2.3 Small Business Taxes

Depending on which business arrangement you select, you can have various taxation choices for your corporation. There could be state-specific taxes that apply to your business. In the state sales tax guides, you can read more about state sales taxes and franchise taxes.

2.4 Open a business bank account & credit card

Personal wealth security necessitates the use of dedicated company banking and credit accounts. If your personal and corporate accounts are combined, your personal properties (such as your house, vehicle, and other valuables) are put at risk if your company-issued. This is referred to as piercing the corporate veil in business law. Furthermore, learning how to create company credit will help you receive credit cards and other borrowings under your business's name (rather than your own), lower interest rates, and more credit lines, among other advantages.

2.5 Open a business bank account

This protects your assets from those of your business, which is essential for personal wealth security, as well as making accounting and tax reporting simpler.

2.6 Get a business credit card

It will help you achieve the following benefits:

It builds the company's credit background and will be beneficial for raising capital and profit later on.

It lets you differentiate personal and business expenditures by placing all of your business's costs under one account.

Set up business accounting

Understanding your business's financial results includes keeping track of your different costs and sources of revenue. Maintaining correct and comprehensive reports also makes annual tax filing even simpler.

2.7 Obtain necessary permits and licenses

Failure to obtain required permits and licenses will result in hefty fines or even the closure of your company. If you intend to market homemade soaps, you must first acquire a business license.

2.8 State & Local Business Licensing Requirements

Operating a handmade soap company can necessitate the procurement of some state permits and licenses. Furthermore, several states have varying laws governing the manufacturing of cosmetics and other body care goods. Visit the SBA's guide to state licenses and permits to read more about your state's licensing criteria.

2.9 Labor safety requirements

It is essential to comply with all Occupational Safety and Health Administration protocols. Pertinent requirements include:

Employee injury report

Safety signage

2.10 Certificate of Occupancy

A Certificate of Occupancy is normally required for businesses that operate out of a specific location (CO). All requirements concerning building codes, zoning rules, and local requirements have been followed, according to a CO. If you're thinking about renting a space, keep the following in mind:

Securing a CO is normally the landlord's duty.

Before signing a contract, make sure your landlord has or can get a legitimate CO for a soap-making operation.

A new CO is often needed after a significant renovation. If your company will be renovated before opening, add wording in your lease agreement that specifies that lease payments will not begin before a valid CO is issued.

If you intend to buy or build a place:

You would be responsible for securing a legal CO from a local government body.

Review all building codes and zoning standards for your soap-making business's place to ensure that you'll comply and eligible to get a CO.

2.11 Trademark & Copyright Protection

It is wise to protect your interests by applying for the required trademarks and copyrights if you are creating a new product, idea, brand, or design. The essence of legal standards in distance education is continually evolving, especially when it comes to copyright laws. This is a regularly revised database that can assist you with keeping on top of legal specifications.

2.12 Get business insurance

Insurance, including licenses and permits, are necessary for your company to run safely and legally. In the case of a covered loss, corporate insurance covers your company's financial well-being. There are several insurance schemes tailored for diverse types of companies with various risks. If you're not sure what kinds of risks your company might face, start with General Liability Insurance. This is the most popular form of coverage required by small companies, so it's a good place to start.

2.13 Learn more about General Liability Insurance

Workers' Compensation Insurance is another essential insurance scheme that many companies need. When your company hires staff, your state may mandate you to carry the Workers' Benefits Package.

2.14 Define your brand

Your company's brand is what it stands for, as well as how the general public perceives it. A good name would set the company apart from the market.

How to promote & market a soap making business

Look for areas where you can stand out. Try having a larger-than-usual bar of soap or one that is formulated to last longer. Perhaps you should market a six-pack of sampler soaps in smaller sizes so that your customers can check out your whole product range and pick their preferences. Consider an uncommon fragrance or texture additive for applying to your soaps to make them stand out. When you've found a winning design, publicize it on your website and social media. Also, if you're showing your soaps at an exhibition, bring some unwrapped samples of your entire product line so consumers can touch them, see what they're made of, feel their textures, and experience the various scents.

How to keep customers coming back

bear in mind that you're offering an aesthetic experience. Make sure your logo, labels and packages, and the name of your product line all cater to consumers looking for a low-cost luxury experience. One benefit is that the more your consumers like your stuff, the faster they can consume it and require more. Ensure that you retain contact with your clients and that they are aware of how to contact you. Request email addresses from all of your clients to obtain their approval to send out a monthly e-newsletter or catalog. It's important not to bother someone with so many promotional newsletters, but a monthly newsletter will keep consumers updated on all of the new items you have to sell. You might want to add a toll-free phone number for orders as your company expands.

Establish your web presence

Customers can learn more about your business and the goods or services you deliver by visiting your website. One of the most successful ways to build your web presence is through press releases and social media.

2.15 Soap Making Plan

If you live in the jungle and love your body odor, you would not need soap. It is a regular need and one of the common goods. As a result, soap has a huge demand. There are various varieties of soaps available due to the wide range of skin types. Soaps are manufactured in a multitude of ways to suit the needs of all. One of the most promising FMCGs is soap production. Perhaps this is why so many people are drawn to this sector year after year. Every day, in a country like India, there is a massive demand for soap. However, there are only a few competitors in the business. We have a few ideas for you if you want to launch your own soap company. Let's get this started.

Tips for soap making using the cold process method

Soap making is easy at the most fundamental level. The cold process approach is the most common way to produce soap. It's "cold" because the ingredients aren't heated before being combined. Using the "hot process" technique, you can make soap with heat. We will use the cold process. Soap is made by mixing fats and oils with a lye and water solution in the most basic form. Soap is made from a combination of water, lye, fats, and oils. The fun starts as you change the components and quantities of the various materials. But, to keep things simple, note that soap is essentially a solution of fats and oils, lye, and water. It's as plain as that.

Is making soap without lye possible?

Is it possible to produce soap without lye? Not at all. Soap bases that can be heated and poured into molds can be purchased. You didn't have to use lye to make the base as everyone else did. However, you have no idea what's in those bases. Sodium hydroxide is the lye used to produce bar soap. Soft soaps are made of potassium hydroxide. Leaching lye from wood ashes is an easy way to create it. This form of lye results in a smoother soap. Unless you have access to a chemical supply house, lye is typically difficult to come by locally. It is, however, simple to put an order. Lye is highly caustic, and it can sear the skin and strip color from whatever surface it comes into contact with. If it gets into your eyes, it will blind you. This is a toxic drug and can never be used in a place where children may reach it. Adults, on the other hand, would have no trouble with the lye if they take simple precautions. When dealing with lye, please wear safety goggles. Long sleeves and protective gloves are also recommended. Leave lye or lye mixtures unattended at all times. Uncured soap should be used similarly to lye.

Fats and oils required for making the cold process soap

Another fundamental to producing soap can be found here. To turn oils and fats into soap, different quantities of lye are needed. Every fat that is likely to be used in soap making has a known amount of time it takes to turn oil or fat into soap. Simply look up the amount of lye needed to produce soap from a certain oil in a table. The volume of lye used in each recipe is then determined based on the oils used. Using a little less lye than is needed to transform all of the oils into soap. This is achieved as a precautionary step to ensure that all of the lye is absorbed during the process. The lye discount is the volume of lye used that is reduced. It's normal to use around 5% less lye than is needed to completely transform the oils into soap. Coconut, palm, and olive oils are the most common oils used in soap making. If you just use those three oils to make soap, you will make amazing results. Each of these oils has its collection of characteristics that make it useful as a soaping oil. You can produce a soap with only one of the oils, but the results won't be as strong as if you used all three. This is why. If you want a lot of bubbles in your soap, coconut oil is the way to go. It's the root of a slew of big, light bubbles. However, soap made entirely of coconut oil cleans so well that it extracts much of the oil from the skin, leaving it dry. This is why it can only account for about 30% of the soap oils. Palm oil is important for hard, long-lasting bars, but it isn't as clean or bubbly as coconut oil. This fat is often referred to as "vegetable tallow," but it is similar to beef tallow in any way. If you don't want to eat meat fats, use them instead of beef fat. Then you should ask about olive oil. Just olive oil is used to produce castile soap conventionally. If you've ever used this form of soap, you know how good it is as a skin conditioner. It's amazing. However, if olive oil is the only oil used in the soap, the effect is tiny little bubbles and bars that fade away quicker than you'd like. As a result, this type of oil is only used to make up about 40% of the oils in a recipe. Granted, soap can be made from almost any form of fat or oil, and there are several alternatives.

Adding ingredients for premium luxury results

If you choose to use other oils, just apply a small amount during the final stages of the soap-making process. you'll find that you can use almond oil in your example recipe. Simply raise the amount of olive oil in the formula and leave out the almond oil. It was chosen because it brings a little more to the bar's feel and quality. Soap can be used for a lot more than just producing pure soap. All of the additives are what make soap production so exciting. Clays, natural oils, medicinal products, colors, patterns, and a slew of other alternatives are available as additives. The first step to perfect soap is to get the fundamentals correctly, which can be achieved fast and effectively. After learning the fundamentals of soap manufacturing, the soap manufacturer progresses to using a range of exotic ingredients.

How to make soap?

We'll go into the fundamentals of how the soap is made. Bear in mind that this is just the first step. Following that, you may need additional materials and a special recipe to distinguish the product from competitors.

Ingredients

Given below are the following ingredients that would be required for preparing soap:

Take 2/3 cup of coconut oil (that will create lather) and the same amount of olive oil. Moreover, 2/3 cup almond, safflower oil, or grape seed will also be needed.

Then you'll need a quarter cup of lye, which is sodium hydroxide in its purest form. Finally, you'll require 3/4 cup of cool water that is distilled or pure.

You'll also need oatmeal, aloe vera gel, cornmeal, clay, salt, and any other items you choose to use.

Instructions

Listed below are the step-by-step directions that you must follow in the preparation of soap:

Put on your gloves and pour lye and water into a canning jar. Allow them to sit for a few minutes after they've been stirred gently and the water has begun to clear.

Now pour in the oil from the pint jar. Then Stir well, then put the jar in a warm pan of the water that is bubbling (and/or you may microwave it, when you do, place temperature to one hundred and twenty degrees F).

Remove the lye after that is finished. Allow the lye to cool. Remove pint jar & allow your oil to cool as well. Both can achieve a temperature of 95 to 105 degrees Fahrenheit. If the temperature drops below 95 degrees F, the soap will begin to crumble.

Pour them into a mixing bowl until they've hit the ideal temperature and whisk until fully combined. After stirring for five minutes, mix it with an immersion blender.

Then, to make the soap special, apply herbs, essential oils, & any other things that go with it. They can be thoroughly combined so they appear coarse. Place them in molds & cover with a towel.

After a day check the soap and let it stay for an additional 12 to 24 hours if it's either warm or soft.

When the soaps are fully cured, wrap them in the paper wax & lock them in an airtight jar for a week. Since this soap contains oil on its own, we'll need an airtight jar. As a consequence, interaction with air will cause it to pick up debris and dust.

Soap making machine and price

 fiber covered mixing machine will cost you at least about US$ 1000. This price includes a fiber-covered mixing machine capable of producing 200 kilograms of detergent powder.

Where to get soap making machine?

Online, you can buy a soap-manufacturing machine. Soap manufacturing machines are available from several online retailers. These websites sell the requisite appliances, including the microwave, blender, wrapper, mold, and labeler, also the main device. A soap-making unit, for example, can be bought for the US $ 5000. This item can be used to produce toilet soaps and detergent cakes. If you're searching for something less costly, say under the US $ 1500 apiece, you can easily find it on the market. It can be used to produce soap for bathing purposes. There are also other products of varying price points. However, the budget may start at one dollar an item. You'll get a good detergent maker for this amount.

Soap making raw material and price

The Soap-making ingredients may be bought for a very cheap price. It is much less costly if you buy them in bulk. If you may get the price correct upfront, the rest of the company will be a breeze later on. As a consequence, we prefer bulk raw materials. Alkali and fat are the two main raw materials used to produce soap. the raw material which is most commonly used in soap manufacture is sodium hydroxide. Potassium hydroxide, on the other hand, maybe used. The latter makes a soap that is more soluble in water. As a result, potassium hydroxide creates "warm soap." Locally, raw products are available at a reduced quality. You can discover raw materials for manufacturing soaps online or in your neighborhood with a fast Google search. People typically buy this locally so it cuts the price even further. Rest assured that rates can differ depending on your needs. It depends solely on how much you're making & how much of the raw material you'll need. Caustic soda costs about US $ 150-250 per metric ton on the market. The price of 1000 grams of laundry soap ranges between US$1 and $1.25.

Soap making formulae

legitimate chemical formulae for the soap's $C_{17}H_{35}COONa$. Its chemical name is thus sodium stearate. However, it is important to note that it's for the common soap that is used for personal purposes only. For the detergents, there are normally long chains of carboxylic acid as well as sulfonate salts or ammonium salt.

2.16 Soap selling process

Let us now go through the packaging, distribution, marketing, and promotion processes.

Colorful wrappings

Choose a bright & eye-catching label that will guarantee that the product is noticed. To set it apart from the competition, style it & use the proper design.

Branding

Make the most of this opportunity to build your brand through packaging. Choose a design that you think best reflects your business.

Go simple

Today's entrepreneurs aim for simplicity. Examine the performance of POP displays as well. If they don't live up to your standards, it's time to make a change.

Soap marketing strategy

You can use the following strategies for marketing soap:

Email marketing

And the ones who also sign up for your offer are truly interested in the soaps, email marketing is the perfect way to market. It's also becoming highly customizable and cost-efficient these days.

Blogging

The next logical move is to start blogging. You'll need to hunt down some prominent bloggers who may help you spread the word about the business. You may even invite them to write a review on their blog about a sample of the product.

Social media

Due to availability of the social media, it is now easier to create a brand. Furthermore, guess what? It's the shortest and least expensive alternative. The secret is to make something go viral. this could be the merchandise, online presence, or your ads.

2.17 Soap making supplies

To make it function properly, you'll need some modernized tools equipment, as well as a lot of the space. You will need to find rental space to make the soap. Some of the typical things you'll need to get started include cyclone, mixing vessels, perfumers, blowers, reactors, furnaces, weighing scales, and blenders.

2.18 Marketing area for soap

The marketing region you select will be decided by the audience you're targeting. You would be able to segment your customers depending on age and demographic in social media marketing. Your marketing field can be decided by the type of soap you sell. If you're selling detergent cakes, for example, they're mainly aimed at homemakers of different ages. As a consequence, you will show the commercial depending on age & gender. Marketing is successful on a variety of measures. It simply depends upon whether you've online or a physical company. In any case, it's better to entrust this to a practitioner.

2.19 Total investment

The Investment isn't based on raw materials. Just As mentioned above, different raw materials are used for personal and detergent soaps. Therefore investment will be different for each category.

You must take into consideration the size and place of the business for starting the business. So You need minimum money of US $ 20,000to purchase the machinery along with primary raw materials –if you decide to start with little.

Raw materials shall cost the US $ 2500 per month. Moreover, making unit rentals would charge not less than the US $ 1000 per month. In addition to the above-mentioned costs, the salary of the plant manager is expected to be around the US $ 500. Equipment shall cost around the US $ 10,000 or more.

In addition to the above prices, you need the US $ 500 for license & registration. Moreover, you will need another US $ 800 to cover the accidental coverage. the Marketing might cost you approximately US $ 500 per month.

2.20 Selling price

Supply, materials, brand, packaging, and other factors impact soap pricing. When you're only starting, keep the rates comparable to those of your rivals.

Prices are determined by several factors. A lower-cost soap is generally assumed to be of lower quality. As a result, we won't keep prices very low about market prices.

Additionally, too high prices could decrease overall demand. As a consequence, we will arrive at the golden middle & retain it just marginally, so at all, below current levels.

2.21 Profit margin

Measure profit margins through factoring in your annual manufacturing expenses. You must also remember manpower, raw materials, utilities, and maintenance costs.

This business has a high-profit margin, but it also has a lot of competition from well-known brands. As a result, profit margins would be dictated by the price of the goods.

Know more about your rivals' prices and, as a result, determine which would give the greatest return – find the "golden value point" for the sales.

2.22 Precaution

It is important to obtain insurance. it is why, in addition to other necessities, insurance must still be part of the investment.

Another crucial step's to understand the company's legal framework. Obtain both the "consent to establish" and "consent to operate."

2.23 Risk

In the soap industry, the risk is not creating a large enough brand to compete with the rivals. There are a lot of competitors in the business, so making a name for your company can be challenging.

Another danger is that the company will collapse due to a lack of consumer awareness. To run a good soap company, you must first select the right market.

2.24 Conclusion

Soap production, as satisfying as this is, necessitates thorough study and measured risk-taking. Seeking your niche and launching a company are just simple activities. However, careful preparation and intervention are necessary to make this a success. Make sure you don't undersell yourself & that you also stand out.

2.25 Advantage of starting a soap making business at home

Soap making requires little investment to start with

The supplies needed to make soap can be easily acquired

Equipment required can also be easily acquired

It is comparatively much easier to learn the making of soap

There is already good demand for handmade soap and people are willing to purchase handmade soap,

You can easily specialize in your particular field

It's rather easier to make soap that is both distinctive and different from the existing ones

You can create other products that can gel in with your existing products

You can generate handsome profits by selling soap

It is very easy to locate a market for the soaps

2.26 How Much Money Can You Make Making Soap?

That's a tough question to answer because so much depends on you. And, just to be clear, producing soap is not lucrative. Of course, the money is in the soap sales. To make money selling a product, much as with any other business endeavor takes a lot of time and commitment.

CHAPTER 3: Start a Profitable Candle Making Business

Candlemakers are extremely professional artisans who pay particular attention to the sensory aesthetics of their products and experienced business people who know how to entice consumers with innovative marketing tactics. Learn how to launch a candle-making company of your own.

3.1 Steps for starting a candle making business

You've uncovered the ideal market opportunity and are now prepared to take the next step. There's more to launching a company than simply filing papers with the government. We've put together a list of steps to help you get started with your candle-making business. These measures will ensure that the new company is well-planned, legally compliant, and properly registered.

Plan your business

As an entrepreneur, you must have a well-thought-out strategy. It will assist you in figuring out the additional data of your organization and uncovering any unknowns. Given below are some key points to consider:

What are the startup and recurring costs?

Who is the targeted audience?

What is the maximum price you will charge from the customers?

What would you name your company?

What are the costs involved in opening a candle-making business?

You will be able to start your business at home, based on local zoning rules, making use of your kitchen heat source as well as utensils. Many online retailers, including Candle Science and CandleChem, offer a starter kit of items. To start, your candle materials shouldn't cost more than a few hundred dollars. This includes:

Paraffin, gel, soy, beeswax, or other wax

Wicks

Jars, tins, or other containers (though bear in mind that if you're just selling pillar candles, you won't need containers)

Fragrance oils

Coloring agents

Packaging materials

Transportation costs of raw goods in and finished products out

Web growth, which can cost anywhere from nothing to a few hundred dollars based on the expertise in the industry and at least properly contributes to some other start-up costs. A booth will cost $100 per day if you intend to showcase your goods at different exhibits and festivals, plus you'll have to pay for fuel and other travel expenses. You can also contact an insurance provider first. Since there is a chance of a fire accident, you can ensure that your company is fire-proofed and that you have a fire extinguisher onboard. You can also have an initial consultation with a lawyer to decide what licenses or permits are required in your region.

What are the ongoing expenses for a candle-making business?

The majority of the business revolves around different varieties of wax, your containers, and paint and scent additives. You can purchase these goods in bulk at lower per-unit prices once you've established your business model is viable. Wax, for example, can be ordered in 25-pound sizes for as little as a dollar per pound. Wicks are sold in 100-foot spools. Bulk amounts of containers, such as glass pots, mason jars, and tins, are also available.

Who is the target market?

Anyone who needs candles is your end customer. Some may have specific concerns, such as lights in the case of a power outage, and others are searching for a more sensory experience. Churches that use candles to decorate prayer offerings or stores that wish to bring a dramatic effect to their showrooms are often fantastic consumers. You may also approach resellers that can order the goods in vast quantities. Shop owners from the neighborhood and beyond will be among them. Customers like these are usually seen at arts and crafts shows. Try renting stalls at arts and crafts shows, flea markets, festivals and fairs, and other similar venues if you love seeing your customers face to face in an atmosphere where they can truly appreciate the aesthetics of your goods.

How does a candle-making business make money?

Candlemakers market candles to customers directly or indirectly through resellers such as boutiques, gift stores, and other arts and crafts shopping outlets. Since candle making is such a wide field, differentiate yourself by the types of candles you sell (pillar, floating, votive, tea, etc.) or the quality of your offering. Experiment with scents, textures, and molds to come up with something unique that is worth premium pricing. Furthermore, for optimum profit margins on your sales, you can still be on the lookout for low-cost raw material suppliers. To widen your target audience, think of related products or candle styles.

3.2 How much can you charge customers?

Your goods could sell for as little as a few bucks or as much as $20 or more per unit. Pricing will be dictated by the nature and reach of your product line, as well as your target market, marketing plan, and competitiveness. If you want to be the lowest vendor, make sure you're buying your raw materials at a discount and that you're still aware of what your rivals are charging. To save the most cost per unit, you'll want to buy wax, wicks, coloring agents, scents, and other products in bulk. If your goal is to market a higher-end product line, price is less important as long as your goods are visually pleasing. If you find a retail reseller that can move a lot of your product, you might want to consider giving deep discounts on prices.

How much profit can a candle-making business make?

Profit margins of 50% or more are not out of the question. While the cost of materials is not especially high, make sure you have the resources to devote to making your company profitable.

How can you make your business more profitable?

Consider expanding the product offerings once you've perfected the principles of candle-making. For example, learning how to mold or carve candles into any shape will improve the cost and revenue potential. Alternatively, you might start selling fancy oil lamps made from liquid candles. Find scented soaps and incense as well as other sensory items. You might be able to learn how to make these additions to your expanding product line, or you might be able to figure out where to purchase them for resale. Consider offering candle-making lessons if you have the requisite space in your workshop. You might contact the local community center or community college in this effort and see if they'd be involved in adding your class to their program. Finally, is the company prosperous enough that you might consider franchising it? You have to give this important factor a thorough consideration if you want to enhance your profits.

What will you name your business?

Choosing the correct name is vital and daunting. If you own a sole proprietorship, you should start using a separate company name from your own. We suggest reviewing the following references before filing a company name:

The state's business records

Federal and state trademark records

Social media sites

Web domain availability

It's important to get your domain name registered before anyone else. After registering a domain name, you should consider setting up a professional email account (@yourcompany.com).

Form a legal entity

The sole proprietorship, partnership, limited liability company (LLC), and corporation are the most traditional corporate structures. If your candle manufacturing company is used, creating a legitimate business entity such as an LLC or corporation prevents you from being found legally accountable.

Register for taxes

Before you can start doing business, you'll need to apply for several state and federal taxes. You would need to apply for an EIN to pay for taxation. It's very basic and free.

Small Business Taxes

Depending on which business arrangement you select, you can have various taxation choices for your corporation. There could be state-specific taxes that apply to your business. In the state sales tax guides, you can read more about state sales taxes and franchise taxes.

Open a business bank account & credit card

Personal wealth security necessitates the use of dedicated company banking and credit accounts. If your personal and corporate accounts are combined, your personal properties (such as your house, vehicle, and other valuables) are put at risk if your company-issued. This is referred to as piercing the corporate veil in business law. Furthermore, learning how to create company credit will help you receive credit cards and another borrowing under your business's name (rather than your own), lower interest rates, and more credit lines, among other advantages.

Open a business bank account

This protects your assets from those of your business, which is essential for personal wealth security, as well as making accounting and tax reporting simpler.

Get a business credit card

It will help you achieve the following benefits:

It builds the company's credit background and will be beneficial for raising capital and profit later on.

It lets you differentiate personal and business expenditures by placing all of your business's costs under one account.

Set up business accounting

Understanding your business's financial results includes keeping track of your different costs and sources of revenue. Maintaining correct and comprehensive reports also makes annual tax filing even simpler.

Labor safety requirements

It is essential to comply with all Occupational Safety and Health Administration protocols. Pertinent requirements include:

Employee injury report

Safety signage

Certificate of Occupancy

A Certificate of Occupancy is normally required for businesses that operate out of a specific location (CO). All requirements concerning building codes, zoning rules, and local requirements have been followed, according to a CO. If you're thinking about renting a space, keep the following in mind:

Securing a CO is normally the landlord's duty.

Before signing a contract, make sure your landlord has or can get a legitimate CO for a soap-making operation.

A new CO is often needed after a significant renovation. If your company will be renovated before opening, add wording in your lease agreement that specifies that lease payments will not begin before a valid CO is issued.

If you intend to buy or build a place:

You would be responsible for securing a legal CO from a local government body.

Review all building codes and zoning standards for your candle-making business's place to ensure that you'll comply and eligible to get a CO.

Trademark & Copyright Protection

It is wise to protect your interests by applying for the required trademarks and copyrights if you are creating a new product, idea, brand, or design. The essence of legal standards in distance education is continually evolving, especially when it comes to copyright laws. This is a regularly revised database that can assist you with keeping on top of legal specifications.

Get business insurance

Insurance, including licenses and permits, are necessary for your company to run safely and legally. In the case of a covered loss, corporate insurance covers your company's financial well-being. There are several insurance schemes tailored for diverse types of companies with various risks. If you're not sure what kinds of risks your company might face, start with General Liability Insurance. This is the most popular form of coverage required by small companies, so it's a good place to start.

Define your brand

Your company's brand is what it stands for, as well as how the general public perceives it. A good name would set the company apart from the market.

How to promote & market a candle making business

The first and most crucial step is to decide who you intend to reach. Is your average customer a cost-conscious shopper, or is she more concerned with the sensory experience? If your target market is the former, you should be able to deliver fair prices. If it's the latter, make sure your product range is well-presented and that your color and scent options are pleasing. Try building an online presence on sites including eBay, Amazon, and Etsy. Since these platforms have a lot of competition, keep the costs as low as possible. There is a slew of other arts and crafts marketplaces, but they aren't as well-known as Etsy (and therefore potentially less populated with competitors). Among them are ArtFire, Big Cartel, and Craft Is Art, to name a few.

How to keep customers coming back

You aim to not only retain buyers but to keep them coming back. Since candles are consumable goods that must be replaced daily, the current consumer partnerships may become profitable over time. As a result, make sure you fulfill their needs so that they appreciate the quality of your goods and know-how to reach you if stocks run out. As a consequence, any order must provide easy-to-find contact information, such as your website, email address, or phone number (or all three). As part of the packaging, you could add a business card or sticker with this detail. Make sure shoppers and passers-by alike get your business card when approaching clients in people, such as at art shows or flea markets. Often, get their names and permission to connect them to an email list you give out, maybe before peak candle-buying seasons like the holidays or Mother's Day.

Establish your web presence

Customers can learn more about your business and the goods or services you deliver by visiting your website. One of the most successful ways to build your online presence is through press releases and social media.

Top of Form

Bottom of Form

Is this Business Right For You?

The perfect candle maker is passionate about the craft and has experience in sales and promotion. Candlemakers may start small, with a minimal budget and inventory, in the kitchen and storage room of their home or apartment. Since candles are always thought of as commodity products, you must continually search for ways to brand your line to set yourself apart from the competition. Excellent image photography, a solid web presence, and savvy sales expertise can help you highlight your product line attractively.

What are some skills and experiences that will help you build a successful candle-making business?

The bulk of people get into this business as hobby candle builders. You should appreciate the aesthetics of making candles and related products and have a clear understanding of how to mark your business. You should be familiar with the principles of eCommerce and how to build an online presence. If you sell from a booth at a fair, your display presentation skills are relevant both online (in the quality of your images and written product descriptions) and in physical displays. If you plan to market your product line in person, either to consumers personally or to resellers, personal sales skill is important. You must trust in the goods and be able to convince people to do so as well.

What is the growth potential for a candle-making business?

A good full-time candle maker could earn between $25,000 and $50,000 per year. However, if you sell to a big reseller, you might make more money. Consider franchising your organization once it has become popular enough for others to choose to follow in your footsteps. Candle making is an easy business to launch on your own. However, your ambition likely is to become so well-known that you'll need assistance with crafting, selling, and/or shipping your merchandise. Begin by enlisting the support of friends or family members if required, such as to match seasonal revenue spikes. Don't recruit permanent full-time support once you've been through ample revenue periods to realize that you'll be able to easily reach payroll over the year. Also, contact the accountant to hear about all the hidden expenses.

Candles Pricing

From a business standpoint, you'll need to find out how much you need/want to receive every hour and how many candles you can make in that time. Divide the hourly wage by the number of units (candles) generated to get a figure to add to the basic cost of the supplies used to manufacture each candle until you have these two numbers. Consider the following scenario: You pay $50 on ingredients (not equipment) and can make 20 candles from them. For the supplies, you paid $2.50 per candle. Making candles is a way for you to earn $20 per hour. Since the 20 candles you made took two hours to make, the overall cost is two times $20, or $40. Then you divide $40 by 20 to get a $2 per candle labor rate. When you apply the $2 labor cost to the $2.50 content cost, you get $4.50 per candle. This isn't a great example because you'll need to pay for other expenses like the additional utilities needed to produce the candles and the expense of importing supplies like boilers, pots, and jugs.

How much should you charge for candles?

This is based on the sort of brand you choose to be affiliated with. If you intend to sell bulk candles at a low price, you should expect your company to turn out a huge amount of low-cost candles with a slight but steady profit per candle. Votive candles are cheap and can be ordered for as little as $0.50 each. This approach can be very successful, particularly when several cheap candles are purchased in bulk, resulting in several sales for each customer. The drawback is that you would have to bring in a lot of money to make a big profit. You'll almost definitely need to expand, recruiting someone to help you achieve your broad production goals. Another choice is to create your brand. This means catering to a more discerning public able to pay a premium price for a candle. Some high-end artisanal candles will cost upwards of $200 each. For a brand, you'd have to worry about the packaging theme and what you're encouraging your clients to do with their candles.

3.3 Benefits of candle making business

If you've ever visited a big shopping center, you've probably seen a variety of candle shops. There are whole areas devoted to candles in several major department stores. To give you an example of how strong the candle business is, over 1 million pounds of wax are used to produce candles for the US market alone every year. The candle industry is worth around $2.3 billion a year without additional products such as candlesticks, ceramic pots, and so on. Who makes the most candle purchases? Seasonal holidays account for just 35% of overall sales, making them an outstanding all-year-round investment. Outside of these days, candles are purchased for 65 percent of the year. The most popular motives for buying a candle as a present include a seasonal gift, a housewarming gift, a dinner party gift, a thank you gift, and adult birthday presents. People nowadays believe fragrance to be the most important consideration when buying a candle. Make sure the candles you're thinking of selling have high-quality scents since this can be the difference between success and failure in the candle industry.

Conclusion

In 1969, in a period when India's domestic detergent industry had very few competitors, predominantly multi-national firms, which targeted the affluent of India, Karsanbhai launched Nirma. The detergents were not affordable for most middle-class and poor citizens. Karsanbhai began producing detergent powder in the backyard of his home in Khokra, near Ahmedabad and selling it door to door for Rs 3 per kg, while other brands were charging Rs 13 per kg. Business Standard reported how Karsanbhai came up with a genius idea during the early 1980s, when the Nirma was still struggling with the sales, for drying out market of the goods collecting all the due credits. This was accompanied by a huge ad campaign featuring his daughter singing the iconic Nirma jingle in a white frock. Customers were flocking to markets, only to return empty-handed. Karsanbhai flooded the industry with his goods as the demand for Nirma peaked, leading to huge sales. Nirma's sales peaked that year, making it the most successful detergent, well outselling its closest competitor, Hindustan Unilever's Surf. As Karsanbhai purchased the cement firm LafargeHolcim for 1.4 billion dollars that year, he showed once again that the business appetite is away from over. Mint reported how the deal in Rajasthan and the surrounding area would help Nirma achieve a stronger grip. While a media-shy guy, Karsanbhai, an entrepreneur in the truest sense, has a sharp eye for nation-building. In 1995, he founded the Nirma Institute of Technology, which was followed by the Nirma University of Science and Technology, which was founded in 2003 and is supervised by the Nirma Education and Research Foundation. He initiated the education project Nirmalabs in 2004, aimed at educating and incubating entrepreneurs in India. Karsanbhai Patel received the Padma Shri award in 2010. Just like Nirma, you can also transform your soap and candle-making business into large corporate businesses with the help of your ingenious marketing and creative skills, dedication, perseverance, and unfearfulness of new and challenging situations.

CPSIA information can be obtained
at www.ICGtesting.com
Printed in the USA
BVHW091027220321
603170BV00007B/1174